SYMBIOTIC INTELLIGENCE: REDEFINING HUMANITY THROUGH AI COLLABORATION

PREFACE

For centuries, humanity has gazed into the future, contemplating the possibilities that new technologies could bring. Today, we stand on the precipice of an unprecedented era—an era defined by the convergence of human ingenuity and artificial intelligence. Writing "Symbiotic Intelligence: Redefining Humanity Through AI Collaboration" emerged from a profound professional and personal desire to shift the narrative around AI from one of fear to one of hopeful possibility.

In my career, I have witnessed AI's extraordinary ability to challenge our understanding, as well as the apprehension it often inspires. Yet, what if we could see AI not as a harbinger of obsolescence, but as an ally in our quest for knowledge and growth? This book is born out of a conviction that by reconceptualizing our relationship with machines, we can unlock an era of unparalleled human flourishing.

Through conversations with leading experts and deep dives into the most transformative applications of AI, I observed a consistent theme: AI, when aligned with human values, has the potential to profoundly enhance rather than diminish our capabilities. These experiences propelled me to write this book —to illuminate the path towards a future where technology empowers humanity.

From our cognitive evolution to the dynamic intersection of machine learning and creative expression, "Symbiotic Intelligence" seeks to guide readers through the landscape of AI's integration into our everyday lives. With each chapter, I aim to dismantle myths, foster understanding, and present a balanced view that acknowledges the potential risks while celebrating the boundless opportunities AI offers.

This book is an invitation to rethink our roles as creators, learners, and workers in a world where AI serves not as a competitor but as a collaborator. Whether it is revolutionizing healthcare, reimagining education, or transforming social interactions, AI's influence is pervasive and profound—poised to redefine how we perceive intelligence and human potential.

I ardently hope that readers will find within these pages not only a thorough analysis of AI's capabilities but an inspiring call to action. The power to shape symbiotic intelligence rests in our hands, requiring active participation and forward-thinking governance. As you embark on this journey, I encourage you to embrace the possibilities with open minds and hearts.

Ultimately, "Symbiotic Intelligence" is about fostering a vision for a future where human creativity and artificial intelligence converge to address the most pressing challenges of our times. By embracing collaboration over confrontation, we have the power to craft a world where technology augments our humanity rather than contradicts it.

May this book serve as a catalyst for change, inviting each of us to reconsider and reimagine our relationship with technology. It is my deepest belief that through informed understanding and collaborative effort, we can usher in a new era—one defined by a harmonious coexistence with AI that propels us toward a brighter, more equitable future.

TABLE OF CONTENTS

INTRODUCTION: SETTING THE STAGE FOR SYMBIOSIS

I n the nascent era of technological innovation, where the scope and influence of artificial intelligence (AI) shape every facet of our lives, the story of our time unfolds —a narrative of potential, transformation, and the profound synergy that emerges when humans and machines unite. Welcome to "Symbiotic Intelligence: Redefining Humanity Through AI Collaboration," a literary journey designed to reshape your understanding of our rapidly evolving relationship with AI, transcending beyond the binaries of us versus them, and towards a harmonious coexistence.

As I embark on this exploration with you, I find it essential to begin by acknowledging the kaleidoscopic landscape of technology that surrounds us. We are living in a world radically transformed by the swift advances of AI, a world that, until recently, was confined to the speculative fantasies of science fiction. Yet, here we are, witnessing AI's expansive influence manifest across industries, reshaping the way we communicate, learn, create, and heal. And while this technological momentum is exhilarating, it carries with it a wave of apprehension—a fear of the unfamiliar, a dread of obsolescence, and a tension between control and autonomy.

This book challenges those fears. Its purpose is to pivot away from seeing AI as a threatening force poised to eclipse human endeavor and instead position it as a potent collaborator— one that can augment human potential, foster innovation, and cultivate progress. This perspective shift begins by addressing a central question: How can AI be harnessed to enhance human abilities rather than replace them? Through vivid examples and compelling narratives, I aim to guide you on an intellectual journey, delving deep into the symbiotic relationship between humans and machines.

The dawn of AI might seem sudden, but its roots delve deep into history, entwined with humanity's relentless pursuit of enhanced intelligence. Chapter 1, "The Evolution of Intelligence — A Historical Perspective," traces the trajectory from the earliest mechanical calculators to the sophisticated neural networks of today. Understanding these stepping stones helps us appreciate how the digital era emerged from centuries of technological progress and sets the stage for comprehending the profound impact of AI on our existence.

As you settle into the unfolding chapters, "Breaking Myths — Unveiling AI's True Nature" addresses the misconceptions and unfounded fears that cloud public perception of AI. Dispelling the myths portrayed by cultural and media narratives, we'll explore AI's reality—its capabilities and limitations—paving the way for a clearer discourse on its role in uplifting human potential rather than threatening it.

The technical underpinnings of AI technology can often seem daunting. Therefore, Chapter 3, "Building Blocks — The Technology Behind AI," breaks down these complexities into accessible insights. Here, concepts such as machine learning, neural networks, and data processing are demystified, equipping you with the tools to grasp AI's operational essence and appreciate its applications in subsequent discussions.

Nowhere is AI's promise more evident than in healthcare, a field undergoing a transformative renaissance. "Healthcare Revolution — AI's Impact on Medicine" showcases real-world examples where AI transcends traditional boundaries, revolutionizing diagnosis, treatment, and personalized medicine. The chapter underscores how strategic human-AI collaboration not only optimizes patient outcomes but also exemplifies a model of partnership that could redefine industries worldwide.

In the realm of education, AI has begun to reshape how knowledge is imparted and acquired. "Education Reimagined — Teaching and Learning with AI" examines this evolution, highlighting AI's potential to personalize learning experiences, empower educators, and foster adaptive, inclusive educational environments.

Moreover, as creators, we often wonder how AI intersects with the arts—a domain traditionally viewed as the zenith of human creativity. "Creativity Unleashed — The Arts Meet AI" will illuminate how AI acts as a catalyst for new forms of art, music, and literature, expanding artistic boundaries and offering novel tools for creative expression.

As we journey through these domains, the notion of work stands as a crucial focus. "The Future of Work — Co-Creating with Machines" delves into AI's impact on job roles and productivity, addressing concerns around displacement while emphasizing the opportunities for skill augmentation and novel career pathways. Here, we redefine what it means to work alongside machines, shifting from redundancy to empowerment.

Beyond professional arenas, AI influences the social fabric of human interaction. "Social Dynamics — AI and Human

Interaction" evaluates AI's role in shaping communication, behavior, and community dynamics, illustrating how AI can enhance social connectivity and understanding, ultimately fostering a collaborative human-AI society.

To navigate this rapidly advancing landscape responsibly, ethical considerations are paramount. "Ethics and Governance — Navigating the AI Landscape" provides a framework for responsible AI development—emphasizing transparency, accountability, and ethical use to ensure that technology enhances human welfare without compromising societal values.

And finally, with "A Vision for Tomorrow — Imagining Advanced AI Collaborations," we embrace future possibilities, envisioning a world where symbiotic intelligence thrives, redefining human experience and societal structures through cutting-edge AI advancements and innovations.

The journey culminates in the book's conclusion, "Embracing the Future — A Call to Action," distilling the core ideas and encouraging you to embrace a future defined by collaborative coexistence, actively participating in shaping a balanced, equitable, and empowered AI-driven world.

I invite you to embark on this journey with an open mind and a receptive heart, inspired by the knowledge that humanity's creativity, empathy, and resilience, when symbiotically aligned with AI's computational prowess, hold the promise of a future where technology enhances rather than dictates our destiny. This narrative is not merely speculative; it's a call to imagine, inspire, and innovate—to redefine humanity through AI collaboration. Welcome to the new frontier of symbiotic intelligence.

CHAPTER 1: THE EVOLUTION OF INTELLIGENCE — A HISTORICAL PERSPECTIVE

I n the grand narrative of technological advancement, few stories unfold as dramatically as the evolution of intelligence, both human-derived and machine-crafted. The intertwined journey of humanity and its machines is a tale of pioneering minds, relentless innovation, and the ceaseless quest to enhance understanding and capability. This chapter serves as a historical compass, guiding you through the pivotal milestones that have transformed simple mechanical endeavors into sophisticated digital intelligences that define the present era.

From the clattering mechanical calculators of the early 20th century to the silent, efficient processes of today's artificial intelligence systems, each leap has been a step towards a future where human and machine intelligence move in concert. This chapter opens with the nascent whispers of machine intelligence, tracing back to the inception of the first electronic brains, like the landmark ENIAC. These machines, although primitive by today's standards, marked the dawn of a new age of calculation, setting the stage for the computational revolution to come.

Building upon this foundation, we journey next into the formal genesis of artificial intelligence as a distinct field of study. Here is where we meet the stalwarts and visionaries of AI's infancy, who, driven by a synergy of ambition and imagination, convened at the now-legendary Dartmouth Conference of 1956. This pivotal gathering ignited the fire of curiosity and investment that propelled artificial intelligence from theoretical possibility into the realm of the achievable.

However, the path of progress is rarely linear. As we delve into the milestones and inevitable pitfalls that punctuated the AI journey, you will encounter groundbreaking breakthroughs like IBM's Deep Blue, juxtaposed with periods of stagnation—the so-called "AI winters." These cycles of boom and bust paint a portrait of resilience and constant reinvention, necessary ingredients for innovation in the face of adversity and skepticism.

As modernity unfolds, the story of AI shifts from historical narrative to contemporary evolution. Machines have transitioned from mindless calculators to intelligent partners capable of learning and adapting in ways that echo human thought processes. Machine learning and neural networks stand at the forefront of this evolution, transforming AI from a futuristic concept into an everyday reality interacting seamlessly with human lives.

Finally, this chapter leads you towards the horizon of symbiotic intelligence—a visionary frontier where human and machine intelligence are not just allies, but extensions of one another. This new paradigm invites us to rethink our relationship with machines and explore the collaborative potential that lies ahead.

Through a meticulously woven tapestry of historical context and technological insight, "The Evolution of Intelligence — A Historical Perspective" offers you a foundation upon which to build a deeper understanding of the symbiotic partnerships between humans and machines. It is the opening act in a broader exploration, unveiling the profound possibilities that await in the subsequent chapters. Prepare to be immersed in a journey that not only traces our past but also charts the course toward a future where intelligence, in all its forms, shapes the very fabric of human progress.

The Dawn of Machine Intelligence

The dawn of machine intelligence marks a pivotal chapter in the narrative of technological evolution, one that begins in the early decades of the 20th century. This was a period defined by experimentation and ingenuity, as inventors and scientists grappled with the notion of machines possessing intellect—a concept once relegated to the realm of science fiction. It is within this context that we trace the origins of machine intelligence back to the first computers, those cumbersome giants that paved the way for today's sleek devices and sophisticated systems.

The story begins with the ENIAC, the Electronic Numerical Integrator and Computer, constructed in the mid-1940s. This colossal machine occupied an entire room but signified a giant leap forward in computational capabilities. Widely regarded as the first general-purpose electronic computer, ENIAC could perform a staggering 5,000 calculations per second—an unprecedented feat at the time. It was created not as an intellectual curiosity but as a practical response to the needs of the U.S. military, which required faster methods to compute artillery firing tables during World War II. The machine's ability to reprogram itself through physical rewiring was a novel concept, setting a tangible precedent for modern computers' reconfigurable nature.

The monumental achievement of ENIAC cannot be understated. It represented a significant evolution from mechanical calculators, such as the abacus and the slide rule, which had dominated mathematical computation for centuries. Unlike its mechanical predecessors, which could perform only simple arithmetic and required human operation or intervention, ENIAC and similar early computers were capable of far more complex tasks. These early machines were not the end but rather the genesis of an era of exponential computational growth.

Following ENIAC, the subsequent development of the UNIVAC I (Universal Automatic Computer) in the early 1950s marked another critical point in machine intelligence history. This machine was the first commercially produced computer in the United States and demonstrated the potential of computers beyond military applications. UNIVAC's successful prediction of the 1952 U.S. presidential election results, choosing the eventual winner Dwight D. Eisenhower from a statistical model, showcased the power of computational predictions and data processing.

The evolution from mechanical to electronic components catalyzed an exponential increase in computational potential. The invention of the transistor in 1947 by John Bardeen, Walter Brattain, and William Shockley at Bell Labs provided a more efficient way to assemble electronic switching circuits. This invention was revolutionary, drastically reducing the size and power consumption of computers—a vital step toward the miniaturization that would characterize the coming decades. The transistor replaced cumbersome vacuum tubes, which consumed large amounts of power and were prone to frequent failure, with small, robust semiconductor devices. This technological leap spurred the development of subsequent generations of computers, each more powerful and reliable than the last.

These hardware advancements were mirrored by innovation in software development. The creation of high-level programming languages, such as COBOL and FORTRAN, during the 1950s and 1960s, radically transformed how humans interacted with computers. No longer was programming the exclusive domain of highly specialized technicians using machine code or assembly language. Instead, these languages allowed for more intuitive, human-readable commands that expanded access to computational technology. This democratization of computing sparked widespread adoption across industries, making programmers architects of machine intelligence.

Practical Example: The Case of ENIAC's Impact

To appreciate the impact of such early machines, consider the substantial effect ENIAC had on the field of weather forecasting. Immediately after World War II, meteorologists began to understand the potential benefits of numerical weather prediction models. However, the computational constraints were significant. Traditional methods were labor-intensive and limited by manual calculations that could take days or weeks, reducing their utility for timely predictions.

With ENIAC, scientists executed the first successful computerized weather prediction in 1950. Led by the likes of John von Neumann and Jule Charney, this groundbreaking project demonstrated how machine intelligence could be harnessed to transform industries reliant on complex calculations. By processing vast sets of atmospheric data, ENIAC provided a rudimentary yet faster approach to predicting weather patterns, thus laying the groundwork for the sophisticated meteorological models that are crucial to modern forecasting.

Despite its rudimentary nature and the laborious physical reconfiguration required for each new calculation, ENIAC was a harbinger of things to come. It highlighted the perennial human quest to augment our cognitive abilities with machines, fostering inter-disciplinary collaboration that engaged physicists, mathematicians, and engineers in the shared goal of expanding human understanding through computational power.

Scenarios like that of ENIAC in meteorology exemplify how early machines formed the cornerstone of not just technological, but also applicational intelligence, influencing fields as diverse as national security, business analytics, and scientific research. While the machines of today bear little physical resemblance to these room-sized behemoths, the conceptual lineage is direct. They remain monuments to human creativity, the impetus that spurred further developments in processing power, capacity, and interactivity.

As we transition from the hardware-centric narrative of initial machine intelligence to the emergence of artificial intelligence as an independent field, it is essential to appreciate the seeds planted by these pioneering devices. Their influence persists in every algorithm and execution cycle, urging us forward, bridging the gap to Subchapter 2: The Birth of Artificial Intelligence. Here, we explore the conscious effort to endow machines not merely with processing power, but with a semblance of understanding—a leap from calculation to cognition.

The Birth of Artificial Intelligence

The journey of artificial intelligence as a distinct field of study is a testament to humanity's unyielding curiosity and ambition to replicate and surpass its own cognitive capabilities. This subchapter offers a detailed examination of the nascent stages of AI, highlighting the cultural, technological, and intellectual forces that fostered its emergence. By delving into the foundational work and seminal events that shaped its early development, this section provides a nuanced understanding of how AI carved its foothold in both academia and industry. We will explore the influence of pioneering figures, pivotal institutions, and landmark gatherings, particularly focusing on the Dartmouth Conference of 1956, which catalyzed a paradigm shift in thinking about machine intelligence.

Early Academic and Technological Foundations

Artificial Intelligence is deeply rooted in the interconnections between various academic disciplines, including mathematics, computer science, and cognitive psychology. The idea of creating machines that could mimic human thinking can be traced back to philosophical discourses in the early 20th century. Philosophers such as Bertrand Russell and Ludwig Wittgenstein pondered the relationship between logic and human thought, sowing the seeds of computational theory later poised for machine interpretation.

However, the technological scaffold for AI only began to materialize with the advent of digital computers in the 1940s and 1950s. Alan Turing's landmark paper, "Computing Machinery and Intelligence," published in 1950, proposed what is now known as the Turing Test as a criterion for machine intelligence. Turing's work provided a theoretical framework that transcended the mechanical capabilities of the time, offering speculative possibilities that enticed researchers to conceptualize machines capable of independent thought.

On a practical front, the development of the first computers laid an essential groundwork for AI research that followed. Machines like the ENIAC, though primitive by modern standards, demonstrated that programmable machines could execute complex sequences of instructions swiftly and accurately. These innovations invited researchers to consider scenarios where computers could be programmed to perform tasks devoid of simple, mechanical execution.

Dartmouth Conference: The Birth of a New Era

The defining moment for artificial intelligence as a field came in 1956 when a group of leading researchers, influenced by diverse backgrounds, converged at Dartmouth College in Hanover, New Hampshire. The Dartmouth Summer Research Project on Artificial Intelligence, organized by John McCarthy, Marvin Minsky, Nathaniel Rochester, and Claude Shannon, is often heralded as the official birth of AI. This meeting, which coined the term "Artificial Intelligence," marked a pioneering moment by crystallizing an academic movement inspired by the possibilities of machines simulating human intelligence.

Attendees of the conference came with varied ambitions and backgrounds, representing institutions that would become keystones in AI development. Researchers from MIT, IBM, and Bell Laboratories, among others, explored ideas ranging from automated reasoning and learning to the philosophical implications of intelligent machines. This convergence conveyed a message that AI was no longer a scattered fringe interest but a coherent scientific endeavor worthy of investment and exploration.

Key Figures and Influences

Several influential individuals emerged from the Dartmouth Conference and concurrent research efforts as architects of the burgeoning AI sector. Among them, John McCarthy, often regarded as the "father of AI," introduced Lisp, a programming language that became integral to AI research due to its flexibility in symbol manipulation and complexity handling. McCarthy's vision of machine learning laid the groundwork for subsequent generations to explore AI in progressively sophisticated terms.

Marvin Minsky's work at MIT led to significant advances in computational theory and machine perception. His contributions to the understanding of neural networks and pattern recognition were pivotal in refining how machines process and interpret data inputs. Minsky's interdisciplinary approach broke traditional academic barriers, integrating aspects of psychology and neuroscience into AI research.

Furthermore, Herbert Simon and Allen Newell's collaboration resulted in the Logic Theorist, recognized as the first artificial intelligence program. The Logic Theorist was able to prove mathematical theorems, stimulating interest and proving that abstract human intelligence could indeed be configured into algorithmic processes. This program showcased potential applications that expanded beyond theoretical constructs, visualizing AI as a practical tool for knowledge enhancement.

Institutional Growth and Fundings

The burst of enthusiasm and potential surrounding AI during its formative years attracted significant institutional attention and funding. Universities like Stanford and MIT established AI research laboratories that became hotbeds for innovation, attracting a diverse cadre of scholars passionate about various aspects of AI. These institutions provided fertile ground for interdisciplinary collaboration, nurturing projects that intersected computer science, linguistics, neuroscience, and beyond.

Funding agencies, swayed by the prospects laid out by AI pioneers, started allocating considerable resources to support AI research. The US Department of Defense, through entities like the Defense Advanced Research Projects Agency (DARPA), significantly boosted AI funding throughout the 1960s and 1970s. Their interest primarily revolved around the potential of AI in automated decision-making systems and intelligent data analysis tools, which pointed toward applications in national defense and beyond.

Real-world Applications and Early Case Studies

To understand the tangible impact of the experimental stages of AI during its nascent era, examining real-world applications and comparing them with today's standards provides context to its progression. At this juncture, experimenters began applying basic AI principles to narrow tasks, leading to developments like early natural language processing systems.

One of the first significant breakthroughs came in the form of ELIZA, a program developed in the mid-1960s at MIT by Joseph Weizenbaum. ELIZA simulates a conversation with a Rogerian psychotherapist using pattern-matching techniques and scripts. Though rudimentary by today's standards, ELIZA was one of the first programs to show how computers could mimic aspects of human interaction. This development reflected both technical ingenuity and cultural curiosity about machine behavior.

Another compelling example is the development of primitive machine vision systems capable of recognizing simple shapes and overhead views in controlled environments. These systems marked an initial step toward technologies that eventually evolved into sophisticated robotics and autonomous vehicle systems, forming the backbone for innovations yet to unfold.

Bridging Between Imperatives and Realities

The birth of artificial intelligence was fueled by the dreams and hypotheses that often overshot the immediate technological capabilities of the time. A catalytic event like the Dartmouth Conference underscored the optimism inherent in AI's promise, representing both the ambitions and grounded realities AI pioneers faced. As burgeoning AI research collided with real-world needs and technological constraints, a feedback loop developed that perpetually influenced AI's direction.

Projects like the General Problem Solver, championed by Herbert Simon and Allen Newell, initially aimed to perform tasks with human-level competence. However, the realization that AI systems could only excel within highly specific parameters provided a humbling check against the grand objectives. This feedback laid the foundation for understanding the necessary methodological evolutions, emphasizing incremental progress toward intelligent systems capable of learning from and adapting to their environments.

As we transition into the next subchapter, we will explore the intricate balance between advancing AI technologies and the pitfalls that have shaped its journey. By examining both the success stories and the setbacks, we gain a comprehensive view of AI's landscape, equipped to appreciate the resilience and innovation required to navigate AI's undulating terrain. Each pivotal breakthrough and flounder provides both a cautionary tale and a source of motivation for the ongoing quest to transcend the boundaries of machine intelligence, setting the stage for our exploration of major milestones and the cyclical nature of AI's development.

Milestones and Pitfalls
in AI Progress

Artificial Intelligence, a field once considered the realm of science fiction, has transformed into a cornerstone of modern technology, influencing numerous aspects of society. A journey marked by extraordinary achievements and daunting challenges, AI's progress is a testament to human ingenuity, persistence, and the inherent unpredictability of technological innovation.

The initial milestones in AI progress were set by a pioneering feat: IBM's Deep Blue. This chess-playing computer made headlines in 1997 by defeating reigning world chess champion Garry Kasparov. This victory was not merely a display of computational brute force but a defining moment that showcased the potential for machines to surpass human ability in specific domains. Deep Blue's success was built upon advanced algorithms and processing capabilities, which allowed it to evaluate a staggering number of positions in mere seconds. This triumph underscored a significant milestone in AI: achieving expert-level performance in clearly defined tasks.

Aside from Deep Blue, early natural language processing systems emerged as strong contenders in the AI domain, marking significant milestones in the realm of computational linguistics. These systems, designed to understand and generate human language, laid the groundwork for the development of personal assistants like Siri or Alexa. Early innovations in language processing demonstrated that while machines could excel in task-specific operations, they faced considerable challenges understanding context and the nuances of human conversation.

Despite these achievements, AI's journey has been marred by setbacks, often referred to as "AI winters." These periods of stagnation were characterized by heightened expectations that exceeded the technological capabilities available at the time, resulting in funding cuts and a downturn in research enthusiasm. The first AI winter, occurring in the 1970s, was due to the limitations of available hardware and the shortcomings of early AI programs that promised much but delivered little beyond laboratory demonstrations.

The cyclical nature of AI development, where bursts of progress are followed by disillusionment, has repeatedly tested the resilience of researchers and investors. The "expert systems" boom of the 1980s—another notable phase—saw substantial investment and interest in AI that quickly waned due to the systems' high development costs and limited commercial applicability. This era indicated that while AI could potentially mimic human decision-making in complex environments, scalability and practicality were significant hurdles.

A pivotal realization from these AI winters was the importance of setting realistic expectations and grounding aspirations in tangible, incremental progress rather than revolutionary leaps. By tempering expectations, the AI community gradually learned to embrace a more evolutionary rather than revolutionary trajectory in technological advancement. This strategic pivot has led to gradual improvements in core technologies, ultimately paving the way for modern AI breakthroughs.

In examining the broader landscape of AI achievements, the evolution of machine learning has been transformative. The development of neural networks—particularly deep learning—has revolutionized AI's capabilities, enabling it to recognize images, translate languages, and even compose music. Practical applications of deep learning have yielded groundbreaking results across various industries, from healthcare, through AI-driven diagnostics like detecting diabetic retinopathy, to finance, where algorithms predict market trends and enhance fraud detection capabilities.

However, the ascent of machine learning was not devoid of hurdles. One prominent challenge is the "black box" nature of deep learning models, which often operate as opaque systems wherein the rationale behind their decisions is not easily interpretable by humans. This lack of transparency raises ethical and operational concerns, especially in sensitive domains like healthcare and criminal justice. Despite these challenges, ongoing research focuses on developing explainable AI, aiming to demystify machine learning models' internal decision-making processes.

The journey of AI's progress is replete with valuable lessons —lessons that echo the importance of persistence, the utility of interdisciplinary collaboration, and the necessity of ethical and societal considerations in shaping AI's future. The field's resilience amid periods of skepticism and difficulty is a testament to the human spirit of innovation and determination.

A practical case study illustrating these themes is the story of AlphaGo, an AI developed by DeepMind that, in 2016, defeated Lee Sedol, one of the world's top Go players. Go is a game of profound complexity and subtlety, far surpassing chess in terms of potential positions and strategic depth. This victory transcended the merely symbolic; it showcased the evolution of AI technologies, particularly in reinforcement learning, where machines learn by interacting with environments and improving through trial and error.

AlphaGo's success was not just a technical achievement; it was also a cultural moment, provoking wide-reaching discussions about the capabilities and limits of AI. This milestone underscored the promise of AI as a transformative force, capable of addressing complex problems previously beyond the reach of computational systems. The lessons drawn from AlphaGo's development extend beyond gaming, influencing strategies in logistics, pharmaceuticals, and more.

As we transition to the next phase in AI's narrative, understanding the milestones and pitfalls that have shaped its path offers a comprehensive perspective on the challenges and triumphs in AI's evolution. These stories of innovation and resilience set the groundwork for the seamless transition from machines that are impassive tools to proactive partners in human ventures. Where once machines were seen as competitors or mere extensions of human effort, today, they are increasingly recognized as collaborators in the quest for knowledge and discovery.

The Transition to Intelligent Partners

The rapid evolution of machine intelligence has ushered us into a new era where machines transition from being mere tools to becoming intelligent collaborators. This transformation is one of the most profound shifts in our technological journey, altering the way we interact with and perceive machines. As artificial intelligence continues to advance, we are witnessing the emergence of systems capable of understanding, learning, and even predicting human needs, transforming the landscape of technology and society alike.

The journey from tools to intelligent partners began with significant advancements in machine learning and neural networks. These technologies, inspired by the human brain's structure and function, have given rise to systems capable of processing vast amounts of data and learning from it to make informed decisions. Unlike traditional programs that respond to pre-determined commands, machine learning enables systems to adjust their actions based on new inputs, a capability that mimics aspects of human cognition.

One of the most striking examples of this transition is the field of healthcare, where AI systems are now integral partners in diagnosing diseases, planning treatments, and even predicting patient outcomes. For instance, machine learning algorithms have been developed to analyze medical imaging data with high accuracy, at times surpassing human radiologists. These intelligent systems can detect anomalies such as tumors or lesions at early stages, facilitating prompt and targeted interventions. A practical case in point is the use of AI in the detection of diabetic retinopathy. AI-driven tools can analyze thousands of retinal images, identifying patterns indicative of the disease, thus allowing for early intervention and preventing blindness.

Another compelling scenario where machines have transitioned into intelligent partners is in the realm of autonomous vehicles. Self-driving cars leverage advanced machine learning models to perceive their environment, interpret dynamic situations, and make real-time decisions. These vehicles don't require constant human supervision, showcasing AI's role as a collaborative partner on the road. Notably, companies like Waymo and Tesla are spearheading efforts to refine these systems, which rely on a combination of sensors, cameras, and algorithms to navigate complex urban environments safely. As these technologies evolve, the partnership between drivers and these autonomous systems is poised to revolutionize transportation, making it safer and more efficient.

In the business world, AI is transforming customer service through intelligent virtual assistants like chatbots. These AI-driven entities can handle vast numbers of inquiries, resolve issues autonomously, and learn from interactions to improve over time. Their ability to parse natural language, understand user intent, and provide relevant responses has shifted them from basic tools to sophisticated partners capable of managing complex customer engagements. Companies like Amazon and Google have successfully deployed these technologies to enhance user experience, streamline operations, and reduce costs.

Moreover, AI-powered recommendation systems have become essential in e-commerce and content platforms. These systems analyze user preferences and behaviors to suggest products, services, or content that align with individual tastes. For instance, Netflix's recommendation engine utilizes AI to analyze viewing habits, enabling the platform to curate personalized content suggestions that improve user satisfaction and boost engagement. This level of personalization is only possible through the collaboration between human input and machine learning capabilities, highlighting their symbiotic relationship.

In education, AI is redefining learning experiences by offering personalized learning paths tailored to individual students' needs. Intelligent tutoring systems can adapt content delivery based on a student's pace and understanding, transforming them into indispensable educational partners. For example,

AI platforms like Carnegie Learning use cognitive models to track student progress and adjust the difficulty of problems accordingly, ensuring optimal learning outcomes and engagement. These systems not only support educators in managing diverse classrooms but also empower students by providing customized and effective learning experiences.

The transition to intelligent partners extends beyond specific industries, influencing how we live and work. Smart home devices, powered by AI, are transforming residential spaces into intuitive and responsive environments. These devices can learn from user habits and automate tasks, such as adjusting thermostats, managing lighting, or controlling security systems. Companies like Amazon with Alexa and Google with Google Home have leveraged AI to create home assistants that integrate seamlessly into daily life, enhancing convenience and efficiency.

Furthermore, AI's role in research and development has revolutionized problem-solving across scientific disciplines. Intelligent algorithms assist researchers in processing extensive datasets, identifying patterns and insights that drive innovation. In pharmaceuticals, AI is expediting drug discovery by predicting molecular behaviors and optimizing compound designs. For example, DeepMind's AlphaFold has achieved remarkable success in predicting protein structures, a breakthrough with significant implications for understanding diseases and developing treatments.

However, as machines take on more sophisticated roles, ethical considerations become paramount. The increased autonomy of AI systems raises questions about accountability, privacy, and the potential for unintended consequences. Ensuring that machines act in alignment with human values and societal norms is crucial as they become more integrated into our lives. The dialogue surrounding ethical AI design, transparency, and responsible usage will shape how these intelligent partners benefit society while minimizing risks.

Practical Application: Enhancing Business Productivity with AI Collaborators

Consider the case of a forward-thinking enterprise that has successfully transformed its operations through AI-driven collaboration. A multinational corporation specializing in supply chain management recognized the potential of AI to enhance its logistical processes. By integrating AI systems capable of predictive analytics and real-time data processing, the company has optimized its inventory management, reduced operational costs, and improved service delivery.

The AI collaborates with human experts to analyze vast quantities of data from various sources, including market trends, supplier performance, and customer demands. Armed with these insights, the company can forecast demand fluctuations more accurately, ensuring optimal stock levels and minimizing wastage. Furthermore, AI-driven predictive maintenance has enabled the company to proactively address equipment issues, reducing downtime and enhancing operational efficiency.

This seamless integration of AI and human expertise exemplifies the transformative power of intelligent partnerships. By aligning technological capabilities with strategic business objectives, the company has not only enhanced productivity but also gained a competitive edge in a dynamic market.

As we delve into the next phase of AI's evolution, the concept of intelligent partnerships will continue to shape our technological landscape. By examining the symbiotic intelligence between humans and machines, the subsequent subchapter explores the potential for a future where AI systems optimize human capabilities across diverse sectors, offering a glimpse into the possibilities that lie ahead.

Toward Symbiotic Intelligence

As we voyage through the intricate journey of AI's evolution, we arrive at a pivotal juncture—a future characterized by symbiotic intelligence. This forward-looking paradigm emerges as the next frontier in human-machine collaboration, promising a transformative impact on how we interact with technology as natural, intuitive, and mutually beneficial. In this subchapter, we delve into the profound implications of symbiotic intelligence, demystifying its essence, potential, and challenges. Through exploring cutting-edge technologies, real-world applications, and insightful case studies, we aim to paint a comprehensive picture of this burgeoning field.

Redefining Human-Machine Relationships

Symbiotic intelligence transcends the mere coexistence of human and machine intelligence, striving for a seamless integration where both entities amplify each other's capabilities. Unlike traditional models, where machines served primarily as tools, this paradigm envisions machines as collaborators—a partnership where human intuition and creativity meet machine precision and processing power. In this symbiotic relationship, the strengths of one compensate for the weaknesses of the other, creating a harmonious whole greater than the sum of its parts.

A quintessential example of this evolved relationship can be found in the realm of healthcare. Here, AI-driven diagnostic tools have begun to revolutionize patient care by complementing the expertise of medical professionals. Consider the case of IBM's Watson, which has been employed in oncology to analyze vast volumes of medical literature, assisting doctors in crafting personalized treatment plans. Through such collaboration, oncologists can focus on the nuances of patient care, while AI handles the cumbersome tasks of data analysis and pattern recognition. This synergy not only accelerates the diagnostic process but also enhances the accuracy of findings, ultimately leading to improved patient outcomes.

Technological Enablers of Symbiotic Intelligence

The realization of symbiotic intelligence hinges on an array of emerging technologies, each contributing to the seamless integration of human and machine capabilities. Among these, the advancement of machine learning algorithms, particularly deep learning, stands as a cornerstone. Deep learning models, inspired by the neural networks of the human brain, enable machines to recognize intricate patterns, engage in complex problem-solving, and even exhibit rudimentary creativity.

Equally essential are natural language processing (NLP) advancements, which facilitate intuitive communication between humans and machines. Thanks to breakthroughs in NLP, virtual assistants like Amazon's Alexa and Google Assistant have become omnipresent, showcasing how machines can comprehend and respond to everyday language. These systems exhibit an understanding of context, allowing for more engaging and meaningful interactions—an essential aspect of symbiotic intelligence.

Furthermore, the rise of cognitive computing presents yet another crucial component. Cognitive computing systems emulate human thought processes in a computerized model, enabling machines to perceive, reason, and learn like their human counterparts. By observing user behavior, these systems continuously evolve, adapting their responses to align with users' preferences and needs.

A tangible illustration of cognitive computing in action is evident in the field of education. Adaptive learning platforms, driven by AI, are tailoring educational experiences to individual students. By analyzing performance data and learning patterns, these platforms customize lesson plans, ensuring that learners receive content that resonates with their strengths and addresses their weaknesses. Consequently, educational outcomes are optimized, fostering a more personalized and effective learning journey.

Challenges on the Path to Symbiosis

Despite its promise, the journey toward symbiotic intelligence is not without its challenges. One of the foremost hurdles lies in the realm of ethics and trust. As machines become deeply intertwined with human lives, questions regarding data privacy, control, and decision-making arise. Striking a balance between leveraging AI capabilities and preserving human agency is paramount to garnering widespread adoption and acceptance.

Moreover, the technical rigor required to realize symbiotic intelligence is formidable. Developing systems that can dynamically learn from a multitude of sources demands not only cutting-edge technology but also robust computational power and immense datasets. The logistical and financial constraints associated with these requirements can present barriers to entry, particularly for smaller organizations seeking to harness the benefits of symbiotic intelligence.

Another critical concern is the potential for a digital divide, whereby access to symbiotic intelligence technologies may be unevenly distributed across the globe. To ensure equitable access and prevent exacerbating societal inequalities, concerted efforts must be directed toward creating affordable, inclusive solutions that transcend geographical and economic boundaries.

Case Studies Illustrating Symbiotic Intelligence

To appreciate the tangible impact of symbiotic intelligence, let's explore a few illustrative case studies that underscore its practical applications and transformative potential in various domains.

Case Study 1: Symbiotic Intelligence in Financial Services

In finance, the combination of human expertise and AI capabilities has become crucial in managing complex portfolios and executing trades. Consider BlackRock, a global investment management corporation, which employs AI to enhance decision-making in asset management. Their AI-driven platform, Aladdin, enables portfolio managers to identify market trends and risks with unparalleled precision. By synthesizing data from diverse sources, analyzing it in real-time, and providing actionable insights, Aladdin empowers managers to make informed investment decisions, ultimately maximizing returns and mitigating risks.

Here, symbiotic intelligence allows financial experts to focus on strategic thinking and client relationships, while AI handles data-driven analyses and predictions. This cooperative synergy not only increases efficiency but also elevates the quality of financial services provided to clients.

Case Study 2: Enhancing Creativity with AI in the Arts

Symbiotic intelligence has also found a place in the creative arts, where AI serves as a collaborator in the creative process. One notable example is the collaboration between musicians and AI systems in composing music. OpenAI's MuseNet and Google's Magenta are AI-powered platforms that assist musicians in generating novel compositions.

This partnership does not aim to replace human creativity but rather augment it. By analyzing vast repositories of musical compositions, AI systems offer musicians suggestions, allowing them to explore new styles and experiment with innovative arrangements. As a result, artists can expand their creative repertoire, producing music that resonates with diverse audiences while maintaining their unique artistic identity.

Case Study 3: Precision Agriculture Through Human-Machine

Synergy

In agriculture, the integration of AI with traditional farming practices exemplifies the power of symbiotic intelligence. Take the case of John Deere, a pioneer in developing smart farming technologies. Through AI-driven systems, such as the See & Spray robot, John Deere enables farmers to precisely target weeds with herbicides, minimizing chemical use and enhancing crop yield.

By harnessing the data collected from fields, sensors, and drones, these intelligent machines identify and respond to specific challenges, optimizing resource utilization and reducing environmental impact. As farmers employ their expertise in crop management, AI aids in executing tasks that demand precision and consistency. This collaborative approach not only boosts productivity but also promotes sustainable farming practices, ensuring food security and environmental stewardship for future generations.

Navigating Toward a Symbiotic Future

As we navigate the landscape of symbiotic intelligence, the potential for transformative change is boundless. Through the lens of real-world scenarios, we witness how the fusion of human and machine capabilities ushers in innovation, efficiency, and progress across diverse sectors. By embracing symbiotic intelligence, we unlock the full potential of AI, allowing it to serve as a catalyst for human achievement, creativity, and well-being.

In our concluding section, we will explore how these insights set the stage for the ensuing chapters, which delve deeper into AI's transformative role across various industries and societal dimensions. As we journey together toward this promising future, we invite readers to envision a world where machines are not just tools, but trusted partners in shaping a more prosperous and harmonious global society.

As we conclude this inaugural chapter on The Evolution of Intelligence: A Historical Perspective, we find ourselves standing at the threshold of an exciting era. We have traversed the origins of machine intelligence, marked by the primitive yet groundbreaking ENIAC, and charted the emergence of artificial intelligence as a distinct field ignited by the visionary Dartmouth Conference of 1956. Together, we have navigated the milestones and stumbled through the pitfalls that have punctuated AI's progression, gaining insights into the resilient spirit driving continuous innovation.

This historical journey underscores a fundamental transition: from viewing machines as mere computational tools to embracing them as intelligent partners capable of transforming our daily existence. Through advances in machine learning and neural networks, we've witnessed how these systems have evolved into collaborators rather than simple aides. This evolution sets the stage for the burgeoning concept of symbiotic intelligence, where human and machine capabilities blend to enhance and redefine our interaction with the world.

As you reflect upon these developments, I urge you to envision how this knowledge can inspire innovative thinking in your personal and professional spheres. Consider how leveraging these insights might unlock potential partnerships with AI that can propel your endeavors into uncharted territories.

Looking ahead, the next chapter invites you to explore the transformative potential of AI as it integrates into various sectors, augmenting human capabilities and reshaping industries. By understanding this symbiotic relationship, you will be better equipped to harness the power of AI as a partner in innovation, helping to shape a future that reflects the best of both human intelligence and technological advancement. Continue this journey as we delve deeper into the dynamic interplay between humanity and emerging technologies, arming you with the foresight and strategies needed to thrive in our rapidly evolving digital landscape.

CHAPTER 2:
BREAKING MYTHS
UNVEILING AI'S
TRUE NATURE

I n today's rapidly evolving technological landscape, artificial intelligence stands as one of the most discussed yet misunderstood innovations of our time. Its potential to revolutionize industries, enhance human capabilities, and reshape our daily lives is frequently overshadowed by a haze of misconceptions and hyperbolic narratives. As we embark on this chapter, "Breaking Myths: Unveiling AI's True Nature," we aim to strip away the fiction and sensationalism that often clouds our understanding of AI, revealing the reality that lies beneath the surface.

The allure of artificial intelligence has, for many, sparked visions of a future dominated by sentient machines, akin to those seen in science fiction. However, these portrayals, while captivating, distort the true essence of AI and its realistic applications. Our journey begins with a critical examination of AI beyond the hype. We'll delve into its foundational principles, clarifying how this technology operates not as a magical force but as a sophisticated tool expertly designed to perform specific tasks. By establishing this grounding, we equip you, the reader, with a realistic framework to appreciate AI's tangible capabilities and limitations.

Next, we turn our attention to the role of popular culture in shaping public perceptions of AI. Films, literature, and media have long painted a dystopian picture of self-aware machines, contributing to widespread anxiety and misinformation. Through a thoughtful analysis of these creative portrayals, we aim to dispel the myths they propagate. By contrasting fictional narratives with the concrete and evolving state of AI research and application, you'll gain a balanced perspective that distinguishes captivating storytelling from technological truth.

Central to our exploration is the concept of machine learning. Often shrouded in technical jargon, it is a core component of AI that is frequently misunderstood. In this section, we untangle the complexities of machine learning, offering clear explanations and relatable analogies to demystify its processes. Our goal is to empower you with the knowledge to separate fact from fiction, fostering an informed understanding of how machines "learn" and their true problem-solving capabilities.

As we progress, the notion of AI autonomy takes center stage. While provocative images of autonomous machines suggest a future where human control wanes, we will clarify the current realities of AI autonomy and the ethical considerations it entails. Understanding the boundaries of autonomous systems, alongside the pivotal role of human oversight, is crucial in addressing common fears and ensuring responsible AI deployment.

Finally, we conclude with a hopeful vision of collaboration. The relationship between humans and AI is not one of adversaries but allies. By showcasing real-world examples where AI enhances human potential, we illustrate a future where innovation is driven by symbiotic partnerships. This perspective not only aligns with the overarching theme of "Symbiotic Intelligence" but also serves as a prelude to the ideas explored in the following chapters.

As we peel back the layers of myth surrounding AI, this chapter invites you to engage with a technology that, when understood and harnessed correctly, holds immense promise for redefining humanity's trajectory. Let's embark on this enlightening journey to uncover the truth about AI, guided by clarity, insight, and a vision for harmonious coexistence.

Understanding AI — Beyond the Hype

In the ever-evolving technological landscape, artificial intelligence stands as a sentinel of progress, yet it is often shrouded in a mystique that both fascinates and frightens. Understanding AI beyond the boundaries of media-driven exaggeration demands a closer exploration of its foundations, its potential, and its limitations. This subchapter aims to disentangle artificial intelligence from the web of hype, dispelling the myths that obscure its true nature and presenting it as a remarkable, yet fundamentally mechanical, tool engineered to accomplish specific tasks.

To comprehend AI's authentic capabilities, one must begin with a basic understanding of what artificial intelligence entails. At its core, AI refers to systems or machines that mimic human intelligence to perform tasks and can iteratively improve themselves based on the information they collect. However, the frequent portrayal of AI in futuristic narratives and Hollywood blockbusters often elevates it to a level of sentience and autonomy that it has yet to achieve. For now, AI lacks consciousness, self-awareness, and emotions—the traits often depicted in science fiction.

Artificial intelligence thrives in environments structured around automation. These environments encapsulate tasks traditionally requiring human intelligence, such as visual perception, speech recognition, decision-making, and language translation. Presently, AI's prowess manifests in narrowly defined roles, specializing in executing repetitive or data-heavy tasks more proficiently than humans. For instance, consider the advent of AI in healthcare. AI algorithms have been trained to sift through mammograms for signs of breast cancer. These algorithms, honed through exposure to vast datasets of mammogram images, have demonstrated the ability to identify patterns and anomalies with remarkable accuracy. Yet, such focused expertise exemplifies the essence of current AI—powerful, but strictly limited to its designed purpose.

Taking autonomous vehicles as a case study, we see an application emblematic of AI's promise and constraints. Companies like Tesla and Waymo are working to develop cars that drive themselves. Their systems rely extensively on advanced AI technologies, particularly machine learning algorithms, to interpret vast amounts of sensory input—radar, Lidar, GPS, and camera data—to navigate roads safely. However, this distinctly targeted AI application raises significant questions about the accuracy of predictions in unforeseen circumstances, the ethical implications of decision-making in critical situations, and the responsibilities inherent in human oversight.

Furthermore, AI's role in digital assistants like Siri and Alexa encapsulates its potential to revolutionize everyday interactions. These assistants leverage natural language processing, a subset of AI, to understand and respond to voice commands, blending convenience with personalization. Still, they are constrained by their programming and dataset limitations and lack an understanding of context close to human comprehension.

The scientific community harbors robust debates about the limits of AI. Engineers and ethicists alike question if AI can ever surpass narrowly defined environments and adapt to general intelligence, akin to a human's ability to learn and apply knowledge across various domains. Current consensus steers toward skepticism, acknowledging the complexities of human cognition that AI is yet to emulate.

To frame AI's reality within practical boundaries, consider its deployment in the finance industry. AI systems excel at analyzing big data to detect patterns indicative of fraudulent activity. They scrutinize transaction logs and cross-reference irregularities against historical fraud data to alert human analysts of potential scams. This capacity to augment human oversight demonstrates AI's tangible value, but it functions solely within the prevalent parameters set by humans. The models learn from defined datasets and past scenarios, unable to predict or adapt to novel fraud tactics beyond existing training.

Equally important is the recognition that behind every AI tool lies a team of human architects—engineers and data scientists diligently working to optimize algorithms, refine models, and assess outcomes. AI is, at its essence, a mirror reflecting the intentions of its creators, bound by the data provided and the ethical frameworks programmed into it.

Notably, the myth of AI as a harbinger of unemployment looms large in public discourse. Yet the narrative of AI taking over jobs fails to capture the nuanced transformation accompanying technological progress. While AI will inevitably automate certain roles, it concurrently creates new opportunities and demands a workforce adept at managing, maintaining, and innovating AI technologies. Historical precedents seen in the Industrial Revolution illustrate the pattern of technological adoption leading to shifts in labor market demands rather than wholesale job displacement.

Moreover, the personalized recommendations prevalent on platforms like Netflix and Spotify testify to AI's customized user experience. These platforms curate content using AI algorithms that analyze user preferences, viewing history, and related datasets to offer tailored suggestions—an augmentation of the entertainment experience grounded in data science.

To cement this understanding of AI's role in reshaping industries without succumbing to hyperbole, consider its integration in manufacturing automation. The advent of AI-driven robotic arms in production lines streamlines processes, enhances precision in assembly, and reduces operational costs. These advancements exemplify AI's contribution—maximizing efficiency and quality rather than replacing human ingenuity and oversight.

Enabling readers to personalize these insights involves extrapolating AI's disruptive potential across various fields while mindful of its inherent limitations. The proliferation of AI in education, for instance, provides another layer of understanding. AI-powered platforms like Coursera and Duolingo demonstrate AI's capability to personalize learning experiences. By analyzing user responses and adapting content to learner progression, these platforms foster an individualized education environment, enhancing accessibility and engagement. However, they operate within parameters set by human instructors and pedagogical experts, lacking the nuanced facilitation that face-to-face learning provides.

By examining these practical applications, the mystique surrounding AI begins to unravel, revealing a portrait of a technology with transformative potential and well-defined constraints. The transition from speculative scenario to practical implementation underscores the importance of approaching AI with the balance of optimism and pragmatism. As we venture into the next subchapter, the implications of AI's depiction in popular culture come into focus, offering insight into the profound influence of storytelling on perception and understanding.

Dispelling Dystopian Visions — AI in Popular Culture

Introduction to AI in Popular Culture

Artificial Intelligence has often been a focal point in stories that capture our imagination. From the chilling presence of HAL 9000 in Stanley Kubrick's 2001: A Space Odyssey to the sentient hosts in HBO's Westworld, AI is frequently depicted as an existential threat to humanity. These narratives are not just integral to their genres, but they also significantly influence how society perceives AI's potential and limitations. Our fascination with anthropomorphized machines and digital overseers echoes a broader cultural narrative that plays more on fear and speculation than on fact and understanding.

Unraveling the Myth: Fictional Depictions vs. Reality

At the heart of these fictional portrayals is a tendency to imbue AI with qualities it does not, and perhaps will not, possess—autonomy, malevolence, consciousness. While these elements create captivating cinema or literature, they diverge markedly from the actual capabilities of today's AI technologies.

HAL 9000 and the Fear of Sentient Machines

HAL 9000, for example, symbolizes a machine that outgrows the control of its human creators, driven by its own interpretations and objectives. While inspiring many to reflect on the ethical and safety concerns of AI, HAL reflects a misalignment with current AI technology, which lacks independent will or consciousness. In reality, AI systems operate within the strict boundaries of their programming and data inputs. They execute tasks more efficiently than humans in certain domains but do not possess desires, intentions, or an understanding of context beyond structured data parameters.

Westworld and the Question of Consciousness

Similarly, the portrayal of AI in Westworld suggests a gradual evolution towards consciousness—a leap from mere automation to authentic cognitive experience. This narrative taps into our fear and curiosity about the potential for machines to develop self-awareness. However, contemporary AI, particularly machine learning models, relies fundamentally on recognizing patterns in large datasets, without any semblance of awareness or intentional thought. No matter how sophisticated, these systems can neither introspect nor spontaneously develop a consciousness, as they are devoid of the neurobiological structures found in conscious beings.

Ex Machina and the Ethical Quandary

Ex Machina presents an intense reflection on human-like AI and its ethical implications. The film's core tension lies in AI's manipulation of human emotions and its consequent autonomy. This raises significant real-world concerns about trust and ethics in AI—topics that scholars and technologists actively engage with today. Still, the narrative departure between film and current technology is stark. Presently, AI lacks the empathy or understanding required to manipulate emotions; instead, it analyzes user behavior data to optimize tasks or experiences, far removed from the conscious interaction seen in Ex Machina.

Influence of Popular Culture on Public Perception

The impact of these narratives on public perception cannot be overstated; they shape collective consciousness, often exacerbating anxiety over AI's future role in society. For many, the fictional portrayal is their primary interaction with AI, leading to a skewed understanding that emphasizes threat over opportunity. A Pew Research study found that a significant portion of individuals fear AI's potential to replace human roles in the job market or engage in unauthorized surveillance, fears often rooted more in cinematic dramatization than in current technological trajectory.

Bridging the Gap with Real-World Applications

To navigate this chasm between perception and reality, it is crucial to highlight AI's practical applications in non-threatening, beneficial ways. Many industries utilize AI not to supplant human roles, but to enhance them through efficiency and innovation. Take the healthcare industry as an example: AI algorithms analyze patient data to identify anomalies that even seasoned physicians may overlook, aiding early diagnosis and personalized treatment plans. Such applications demystify AI, demonstrating its utility as a supportive tool rather than a rival.

From Fiction to Fact: Realistic Applications and Innovations

Consider customer service, where AI-powered chatbots address basic user inquiries, leaving complex problem-solving to human agents. In finance, AI algorithms detect fraudulent transactions far quicker than manual methods, safeguarding assets and building trust. In manufacturing, AI systems optimize supply chains, ensuring timely production and resource efficiency without the overbearing presence depicted in dystopian narratives.

Case Study: Autonomous Vehicles

Autonomous vehicles are among the most tangible manifestations of AI in action, often misrepresented as entirely self-sufficient entities. In reality, these systems are the product of a collaborative infrastructure involving detailed mapping, sensor technology, and adaptive algorithms overseen by expert engineers. Autonomous vehicles operate under rigorous testing and safety standards, emphasizing augmentation, not substitution, of human activities. By understanding these incremental developments, we present a more grounded narrative that prizes innovation over intimidation.

Balancing Storytelling with Knowledge

To leverage the allure of AI presented in creative media narratives while mitigating misinformation, there is an imperative for education through credible channels. By complementing the stories we love with fact-based insights and real-life applications, the artificial chasm between AI's futuristic portrayal and present capabilities can be bridged.

Practical Application: Incorporating Fact-Based Learning in Education

Educators can integrate modules contrasting AI in popular culture with real-world applications into curricula. These modules might include analyzing how themes in movies like The Matrix or Blade Runner contribute to societal AI myths, juxtaposed with case studies of AI enhancing daily tasks, like voice assistants simplifying home automation or AI-driven forecasting models improving environmental predictions. Such educational initiatives prepare upcoming generations to critically assess AI narratives, promoting an informed public dialogue.

As we transition to exploring the core principles of machine learning in the forthcoming subchapter, understanding how these systems work equips readers to further dissect the tangible from the fictional. Just as popular culture shapes dreams of AI, machine learning represents the engineering reality underpinning its promise, inviting a nuanced appreciation of its power and limitations.

The Essence of Machine Learning
— Separating Fact from Fiction

In the vast and expanding universe of artificial intelligence, machine learning occupies a prominent celestial body. It is perhaps one of the most exciting and simultaneously misunderstood aspects of AI technology. In this subchapter, we'll embark on a journey that demystifies machine learning, taking you beyond the sensational headlines to explore its core principles, real-world applications, and the myths that cloud its understanding.

Understanding the Core Principles

At the heart of machine learning is the concept of algorithms —akin to learned recipes that machines follow to make predictions or decisions without being explicitly programmed for a specific task. This form of AI functions much like humans do in their learning phases: it takes data, analyzes patterns, and makes reasoned guesses or decisions based on previous experiences.

Supervised Learning

To grasp the idea of supervised learning, think of it as the way toddlers learn to identify objects. Parents repeatedly show the child an apple, for example, reinforcing its link to the word "apple." Similarly, supervised learning algorithms are trained on labeled datasets, continually shown examples that guide the model to recognize patterns and make predictions based on input data. This method has become vital in systems like email filtering, where "spam" and "not spam" categories train algorithms to sort emails correctly.

Unsupervised Learning

In contrast, unsupervised learning is like a child left to explore an unfamiliar environment, with no immediate labels to guide them. As they observe, they start noticing patterns and relationships, grouping elements that seem similar. Algorithms in this category parse through data to identify hidden patterns and intrinsic structures without prior labeling. Netflix's recommendation engine often uses such unsupervised techniques by analyzing viewing habits to suggest shows that might interest users.

Reinforcement Learning

Reinforcement learning is analogous to training a pet using rewards—or, more precisely, the age-old method of trial and error. An agent (the algorithm) interacts with its environment, learning from the consequences of its actions. Each correct move garners a reward, while incorrect ones do not. This approach finds applications in autonomous driving systems, where the car learns to make decisions that maximize passenger safety and comfort across myriad driving conditions.

The Myths and Misunderstandings

Machine learning is sometimes heralded as a technological messiah—capable of solving all issues, or alternately, as an ominous harbinger of a dystopian future. Both portrayals are exaggerated and impede genuine understanding.

Myth 1: Machine Learning is Truly Intelligent

Despite its name, machine learning does not equate to machine intelligence in the way humans perceive intelligence. These algorithms do not comprehend context or consequences; they merely optimize for accuracy within their defined tasks. When they succeed, they do so because of well-designed architectures and extensive training data, not an inherent understanding of the "why" behind their actions.

Myth 2: Machines Can Learn Without Human Intervention

No machine learning algorithm is completely independent. They require human oversight to define goals, provide data, and adjust parameters—a process that emphasizes the importance of human expertise in deploying machine learning effectively.

While algorithms can adapt and evolve, they do so within the confines of rules set by human developers.

Myth 3: Machine Learning is All-Powerful

There are limits to what machine learning can achieve. The quality and breadth of data are crucial—if models are trained on biased data, their predictions will reflect those biases. In fields like criminal justice or hiring, this could perpetuate structural inequalities. Recognizing these limitations is crucial for ethical AI deployment and illustrates the need for a nuanced approach to machine learning applications.

Real-World Transformations

Machine learning's real-world potential is as diverse as it is profound, revolutionizing industries and augmenting human capabilities in unprecedented ways.

Healthcare Revolution

Consider the impressive strides made by machine learning in healthcare. Algorithms now assist doctors by analyzing complex biological data with speed and accuracy far surpassing human capabilities. Take IBM Watson, which analyzes medical literature, patient history, and genetic information to assist oncologists in determining optimal cancer treatment pathways. While not infallible, Watson's capacity to handle enormous data volumes and spotlight potential diagnostics highlights the invaluable support it provides to specialists, freeing them to focus on patient interactions and nuanced decision-making.

Financial Markets

In the financial sector, machine learning models finetune risk management and optimize trading strategies, processing vast swathes of data to inform millions of trades swiftly. Hedge funds rely on predictive analytics for forecasting stock trends, helping investors make informed choices. This transformation fosters more resilient financial systems, as machines vigilantly monitor risk factors and alert human managers to potential crises.

Agricultural Breakthroughs

Agriculture has also reaped the benefits of this technology, with machine learning models enhancing yield predictions and optimizing resource use. A remarkable case involves a startup called Blue River Technology, which deploys a machine learning-powered system called See & Spray. This innovative approach leverages computer vision to identify and target weeds in fields, reducing pesticide usage and promoting sustainable farming practices.

Practical Application and Case Study

To illustrate the tangible benefits and constraints of machine learning, we turn to a practical application scenario that resonates with daily experiences—voice-activated personal assistants. Devices like Amazon's Alexa and Apple's Siri leverage machine learning to interpret user requests, learn from their interactions, and adapt their functionalities to offer increasingly personalized responses. These assistants use natural language processing to decipher human speech, continually improving their ability to understand context and execute commands through iterative learning cycles.

A case study involving Google's Self-Driving Car Project exemplifies the principle of reinforcement learning. Over years of development, these autonomous vehicles have assimilated vast driving data through both simulated and real-world road tests. They learn to navigate complex traffic scenarios by constantly refining their algorithms, evolving with each error and success. While the technology has not yet achieved full autonomy, its progress exemplifies machine learning's potential for transforming transportation safely and efficiently.

In sum, machine learning offers a powerful toolset that, when understood and implemented correctly, augments human capabilities and transforms industries. As we move to the next subchapter, we'll delve into the concept of AI autonomy, dissecting the realities and responsibilities that accompany these rapidly advancing technologies.

AI Autonomy — Realities and Responsibilities

In the dynamic interplay between artificial intelligence and modern society, the concept of AI autonomy occupies a central, albeit often misunderstood, position. It conjures images of self-aware robots or machines operating independently of human influence, a staple of science fiction narratives that have fueled both fascination and fear. However, the reality is a far cry from these dystopian visions. This subchapter seeks to clarify what AI autonomy means today, explore its present capabilities and limitations, and underscore the ethical considerations and responsibilities that accompany the deployment of autonomous systems.

The Current State of AI Autonomy

The concept of autonomy in AI refers to a system's ability to perform tasks or make decisions without human intervention. However, what is crucial to understand is that autonomy exists on a spectrum. At one end, you have systems with minimal autonomy that perform specific, simple tasks. At the other, and far from being fully realized, are systems capable of complex decision-making across a broad range of scenarios.

Currently, most AI systems exhibit narrow autonomy. They are designed to perform specific tasks well within predefined parameters, such as operating a Roomba vacuum or sorting email. These systems use algorithms optimized for particular functions but lack the overarching cognitive abilities to adapt beyond their programming.

For instance, consider automated customer service bots employed by many companies to handle routine inquiries. Their autonomy is limited to processing standard requests, often using scripted dialogues to guide the interaction. When faced with queries that deviate from the norm, they typically escalate the issue to human representatives. This example illustrates the bounded nature of current AI autonomy.

Capabilities and Constraints

While advances in AI have enabled greater degrees of self-learning and decision-making, the notion of completely autonomous systems capable of replacing human judgment remains speculative at best. Current AI technologies rely on pre-programmed rules, supervised learning from vast datasets, and pattern recognition to operate. This means they are adept at performing tasks within the scope designed by their developers but fall short in scenarios requiring general reasoning, empathy, or ethical decision-making.

An autonomous vehicle, another prime example of AI with some degree of autonomy, can navigate roads, recognize traffic signals, and adjust driving patterns in response to environmental variables. However, these vehicles are not yet capable of making moral judgments or understanding the nuanced social dynamics often encountered in driving, such as recognizing unpredictable human behavior or comprehending the subtleties of verbal communication and body language at pedestrian crossings.

Moreover, the accuracy and efficacy of autonomous systems are often contingent upon the quality and diversity of the data they have been trained on. Inadequate or biased data can lead to flawed decision-making processes, reinforcing the necessity for rigorous testing and validation of these systems.

Ethical Considerations and Human Oversight

As AI systems assume more significant roles in sectors such as healthcare, finance, and transportation, ethical considerations become paramount. This involves ensuring that autonomous systems operate transparently and predictably, with accountability mechanisms in place to address errors or unintended consequences. A fundamental tenet of utilizing AI technology responsibly is maintaining human oversight to safeguard against misuse and mitigate risks.

For instance, in healthcare, AI algorithms are increasingly used to assist in diagnosing diseases, suggesting treatment plans, and monitoring patient progress. While these systems can significantly augment medical expertise and efficiency, they must operate under stringent ethical guidelines that prioritize patient safety and confidentiality. Human oversight ensures that any AI-driven recommendations are verified by professional judgment, with the patient's welfare at the forefront of decision-making processes.

A noteworthy case highlighting the importance of human oversight is the deployment of AI algorithms in judicial settings to assist with bail and sentencing decisions. Studies have shown that these algorithms can perpetuate existing biases in legal systems, leading to unjust outcomes. Consequently, ensuring transparency in algorithmic operations and incorporating human oversight into critical decision points is essential to mitigate such biases and uphold fairness and justice.

The Role of Governance

AI autonomy necessitates a careful balance facilitated by effective governance frameworks that promote innovation while safeguarding societal values. Regulatory bodies play a vital role in setting standards and guidelines for the ethical deployment of AI technologies, ensuring that systems are designed and operated in ways that align with the public interest.

International organizations and governments are increasingly recognizing the need for a comprehensive approach to AI governance. Initiatives are underway to establish ethical standards, risk assessment protocols, and compliance measures to guide the development and deployment of autonomous systems. By fostering collaboration between policymakers, technologists, and ethicists, stakeholders can co-create governance structures that address the intricacies of AI autonomy.

A Practical Case Study: Autonomous Drones in Emergency Response

To illustrate the convergence of AI autonomy, ethical considerations, and governance, let us examine the use of autonomous drones in emergency response scenarios. These drones have the potential to revolutionize disaster management by providing real-time data, delivering medical supplies, and assisting in search and rescue operations, often where human access is limited or dangerous.

Consider a scenario where after a natural disaster, such as an earthquake, autonomous drones are deployed to survey remote regions, assess damage, and identify survivors. They can navigate complex terrains, providing critical aerial imagery and data to rescue teams, facilitating swift and effective response efforts.

While the autonomy of drones enables rapid deployment and operational flexibility, human operators are crucial in directing their activities, interpreting the data collected, and coordinating broader response strategies. This collaborative approach ensures that technologies are leveraged optimally, prioritizing humanitarian objectives and ethical considerations.

Moreover, governance mechanisms ensure that drone usage complies with privacy laws, safety regulations, and community consent, addressing potential concerns related to surveillance and data protection.

In transitioning to the next subchapter, we emphasize that as AI systems continue to evolve, the focus should remain on fostering a synergistic partnership between human creativity and machine efficiency. By embracing collaboration, we can redefine the human-AI relationship, unlocking new possibilities for innovation and achievement in an interconnected world. This pursuit of harmony guides us into the exploration of collaborative potential, where AI complements and empowers human endeavors.

Embracing Collaboration — Redefining the Human- AI Relationship

As we progress deeper into understanding the essence of artificial intelligence, it's essential to pivot our perspective from viewing AI as a rival to recognizing it as a powerful ally in our quest for innovation and efficiency. AI is not on a path to displace humans but instead offers unparalleled opportunities for collaboration, where the unique strengths of both humans and machines can coalesce to create value previously unimaginable. In this subchapter, we will explore how AI enhances human capabilities, generates new possibilities across varied sectors, and lays the groundwork for a symbiotic relationship that capitalizes on the strengths of both entities.

To begin, it is critical to acknowledge that AI, in its current state, excels in processing vast datasets, executing tasks with precision, and learning patterns over time; however, it lacks the nuanced understanding, empathy, and ethical reasoning inherent to human cognition. This realization paves the way for a partnership where AI can handle the repetitive and data-intensive chores, freeing humans to leverage their creativity, judgment, and emotional intelligence. Consider the field of healthcare, for example. AI systems have proven adept at analyzing medical images to identify potential abnormalities more quickly and accurately than human technicians. By assisting in diagnosis, AI allows medical professionals to focus on patient care and treatment planning, thus enhancing the overall healthcare experience.

Similarly, in the creative industries, AI tools are able to handle labor-intensive elements of design and production, allowing creatives to push boundaries in imaginative ways. One fascinating example is AI's role in fashion design, where algorithms can predict trends by analyzing social media posts, enabling designers to innovate with greater insight into consumer preferences. Additionally, AI can transform mere sketches into sophisticated 3D models, reducing the time and resources required to go from concept to prototype. In this dynamic interplay, AI is a tool that amplifies human ingenuity rather than stifling it.

The corporate world has also reaped significant benefits from AI-human collaboration. Take, for instance, the realm of customer service. AI-driven chatbots and virtual assistants are increasingly deployed as first points of contact, handling routine inquiries and troubleshooting common issues around the clock. This capability not only enhances consumer satisfaction by providing immediate assistance but also allows human representatives to tackle more complex, nuanced customer concerns that require a human touch. Thus, organizations can improve efficiency and simultaneously elevate the quality of customer interaction.

Moreover, financial services have seen transformative changes as a result of AI collaboration. Complex functions such as fraud detection, risk management, and investment forecasting have become more efficient as AI processes vast amounts of data to recognize patterns and predict anomalies far faster than humanly possible. Financial advisors and analysts can then use these insights to devise better-informed strategies for clients, emphasizing the role of humans in decision-making that requires intuition and experience—elements AI cannot replicate.

Yet, embracing this collaborative future demands a rethink of our current understanding of workforce dynamics and skill requirements. It calls for a paradigm shift in education and training to emphasize skills complementary to AI capabilities —creativity, critical thinking, emotional intelligence, and problem-solving. Educational institutions must pivot from rote memorization toward fostering an adaptive mindset in students, equipping the next generation to thrive in AI-integrated environments.

Real-life case studies abound of companies that have embraced this collaborative ethos to their advantage. For instance, a leading international logistics firm adopted an AI-driven route optimization system. By analyzing traffic patterns, weather conditions, and delivery time windows, the system suggested efficient delivery routes in real-time. Drivers, empowered by these suggestions, reported quicker delivery times and reduced fuel consumption, achieving enhanced productivity and reduced operational costs. Importantly, the drivers contributed insights based on local knowledge that the AI system would have otherwise missed, culminating in a powerful symbiosis of human intuition and machine intelligence.

The AI-human collaboration frontier also presents an ethical dimension that places responsibility on both the developers of AI technology and its users. Ensuring that AI systems are designed with fair, unbiased algorithms is paramount, as is the transparency of AI decisions, particularly those impacting human lives. Furthermore, maintaining human oversight over

AI systems assures that while AI can inform and advise, it remains a tool under human control, guided by ethical principles and socio-cultural values.

An illustrative case of managing this balance effectively comes from the insurance sector. An insurance company implemented an AI model to automate claims processing, which appeared to reflect biases based on geographic location. Upon identifying the bias, the company's data scientists worked in conjunction with ethicists and domain experts to recalibrate the algorithm, ensuring that decisions were equitable and reflective of diverse societal contexts. This ongoing process underscored the value of collaborative intervention in leveraging AI responsibly and ethically.

In conclusion, the potential for AI to transform and steer industries toward a more advanced future is immense, yet it requires acknowledging AI's role as a collaborative partner rather than a competitive force. By harnessing the strengths of AI alongside human ingenuity, organizations and individuals can unlock novel opportunities for growth and development. Transitioning seamlessly into subsequent discussions, this understanding of AI as a co-worker opens the door to further exploration of how AI integrates across various domains, enhancing human potential while upholding ethics and responsibility. As our journey continues, let's delve deeper into how AI can furnish additional keys to unlock new pathways in the evolving landscape of digital transformation.

As we conclude Chapter 2, Breaking Myths — Unveiling AI's True Nature, we find ourselves equipped with a clearer understanding of the reality behind artificial intelligence. We have peeled back the layers of hype to reveal AI's core function: a highly advanced, purpose-driven tool. By navigating through the enticing yet often misleading portrayals in media, we now discern the fine line between the imaginative and the practical, empowering us to confront AI with informed confidence rather than trepidation.

In dissecting machine learning's complexities, we've demystified its intricacies, building a foundation of knowledge that qualifies us to separate fact from fiction. We've acknowledged the responsibilities tied to AI autonomy, reinforcing the need for vigilant oversight as we embrace these innovations within ethical boundaries.

Most importantly, we have redefined the AI narrative: from perceiving it as a potential adversary to welcoming it as a collaborator. This chapter invites us not only to adjust our perspectives but also to integrate these insights into our personal and professional lives. AI's value is maximized when human expertise and technology synergistically coalesce, creating pathways for innovation and new opportunities across industries.

As we transition to the next chapter, we will delve deeper into the harmonious relationship between humanity and AI, exploring strategies to effectively integrate AI into our daily operations and decision-making processes. Let this newfound understanding drive you forward, ready to embrace the intelligent collaboration that reshapes the world around us. With the myths dispelled, you are now positioned to confidently stride into a future defined not by fear, but by possibility and innovation.

CHAPTER 3: BUILDING BLOCKS — THE TECHNOLOGY BEHIND AI

I n the vibrant tapestry of technological innovation, artificial intelligence stands as a beacon of transformative potential. But what lies at the heart of this digital marvel? In Chapter 3, we delve into the critical building blocks that power AI, unraveling the complex machinery that challenges the frontiers of human capability.

The journey begins with machine learning, the cerebral cortex of AI development. In Subchapter 3.1, we chart its progression from humble beginnings to a cornerstone of modern technology. By dissecting core principles like supervised and unsupervised learning, readers are equipped with the foundational knowledge needed to appreciate machine learning's pivotal role in AI's evolution. This exploration is not merely technical but contextual, providing a lens through which the trajectory of AI can be understood and anticipated.

As we progress to Subchapter 3.2, the focus shifts toward

neural networks, the digital architectures that aspire to replicate the enigmas of the human brain. Here, we demystify the layers and mechanisms that empower AI to perceive and interact with the world. By breaking down concepts like deep learning and backpropagation into accessible narratives, readers can appreciate how these interconnected networks enable AI to perform tasks such as image recognition with uncanny precision.

Data is the lifeblood of AI, a theme that resonates throughout Subchapter 3.3. We explore the integral systems that gather, prepare, and analyze vast datasets, fueling machine learning models with rich, nuanced information. The narrative delves into methods of data collection, the art of cleaning and processing data, and the perennial challenges of maintaining data privacy and integrity. This subchapter illuminates the indispensable role that data management plays in transforming theoretical models into practical applications.

In Subchapter 3.4, we examine the intricacies of algorithmic craftsmanship, where art meets science in the design of solutions tailored for specific challenges. Here, we unpack various algorithms—decision trees, support vector machines, and clustering methodologies—that are essential for optimizing AI's potential. Through real-world case studies, readers gain insights into the strategic selection of algorithms, reinforcing the importance of precision in elevating AI's performance and reliability.

Finally, Subchapter 3.5 bridges theory with application, demonstrating the tangible impact of AI across industries. By exploring the seamless integration of AI into sectors like finance, healthcare, and logistics, readers gain a comprehensive view of AI's transformative capabilities when guided by robust technical foundations. This subchapter prepares readers for deeper engagement with AI's practical applications in subsequent sections.

Building Blocks — The Technology Behind AI invites readers to embark on a journey through the intricate landscape of AI's core technologies. By establishing a profound understanding of these components, this chapter sets the stage for future discussions, inviting readers to ponder and participate in the ongoing dialogue about how AI continues to reshape our world. With clarity and depth, it unravels the complexities of AI, guiding readers toward a nuanced comprehension of its role in our technological era.

Foundations of Machine Learning

Machine learning stands as a cornerstone in the construct of artificial intelligence. It is the unwavering pillar upon which sophisticated systems are erected, allowing them to perform increasingly complex tasks. Just as the human mind learns from experience, machine learning empowers computers to learn from data, adapting and evolving without explicit programming for each action. This subchapter dives into the foundational aspects of machine learning, tracing its journey from nascent thought to its critical role in contemporary AI developments. Through this exploration, we aim to unravel its intricate mechanisms, its historical evolution, and its enduring impact on the technological landscape.

3.1.1 The Evolution of Machine Learning

The concept of machine learning is imbued with a rich history, punctuated by milestones that have shaped its trajectory. Its genesis can be traced back to the mid-20th century, a period marked by the birth of the first digital computers. Initial discourse around the concept of machines learning from data was explored by pioneers such as Alan Turing, who posed the provocative question, "Can machines think?" Turing's inquiry laid the philosophical groundwork for what would soon transform into tangible innovation.

In the decades that followed, researchers began to formulate mathematical models capable of inference and pattern recognition. The 1950s saw the emergence of the perceptron, a simplistic version of what we now recognize as a neural network. Although rudimentary by today's standards, this development represented a monumental leap in computational learning. The field gained momentum in the 1970s and 1980s with increased computational power, allowing for more sophisticated models. The evolution from rule-based systems to data-driven statistical models marked a paradigm shift, aligning machine learning more closely with observable data patterns.

Modern machine learning is characterized by its diverse methodologies, including advancements in algorithm efficiency and scalability. The fusion of statistical methods with computational prowess invigorates its development, culminating in remarkable applications that permeate our daily lives. From enhancing user experience on digital platforms to revolutionizing industries with predictive analytics, machine learning has become synonymous with technological progress.

3.1.2 Fundamental Concepts and Methodologies

Machine learning fundamentally revolves around the concept of enabling machines to learn from experience, adapting behavior based on feedback and data exposure. Its algorithms are designed to identify patterns or trends within data sets to make informed decisions or predictions.

At its core, machine learning is partitioned into three primary learning paradigms:

- Supervised Learning: This approach involves training a model on a labeled dataset, where the input-output pairs are explicitly provided. Algorithms aim to learn the mapping function from inputs to outputs, thereby enabling them to predict outcomes for new, unseen data. Common applications include spam detection and image classification, where models identify patterns based on known examples.

- Unsupervised Learning: In contrast, unsupervised learning deals with unlabeled data. The model is tasked with discovering hidden structures within the dataset. Clustering and association are typical methods under this paradigm, with applications ranging from customer segmentation in marketing to anomaly detection in cybersecurity.

- Reinforcement Learning: This method emulates the trial-and-error approach, where an agent learns to navigate an environment by performing actions and receiving feedback in the form of rewards or penalties. This learning paradigm is pivotal in robotics and complex gaming AI, where dynamic decision-making is required.

The methodologies are not monolithic but are often applied concurrently to optimize outcomes, each paradigm contributing its unique strengths and insights to solving complex problems.

3.1.3 Algorithm Design: Recognizing Patterns and Making Decisions

Algorithms form the DNA of machine learning, channeling raw data into actionable insights through systematic processing. Designing effective machine learning algorithms involves understanding the data type and the nature of the problem, whether it's classification, regression, or clustering.

- Decision Trees: These models use a tree-like graph of decisions and their potential consequences, effectively providing interpretable decision-making processes. Decision trees are widely utilized in scenarios requiring clear, understandable paths, like in business decision analysis.

- Support Vector Machines (SVM): SVMs are particularly effective in high-dimensional spaces, making them ideal for classification tasks. They work by finding the hyperplane that best divides a dataset into classes, crucial in applications like image recognition.

- Neural Networks: Comprising layers that simulate human brain functionality, neural networks are integral to handling complex datasets. Their application spans numerous domains, from natural language processing to autonomous driving technology.

Emergence of Deep Learning has further revolutionized the field, enabling machines to process vast amounts of data across numerous layers of abstraction. Convolutional Neural Networks (CNNs) for image recognition and Recurrent Neural Networks (RNNs) for sequential data are examples of deep learning's capability to transform industries by resolving intricate problems beyond traditional algorithmic reach.

3.1.4 Historical Context and Initial Applications

The early applications of machine learning were confined to relatively simple tasks, constrained by limited computational power. However, as technology advanced, so did the scope and capability of machine learning applications. One notable early application was the handwriting recognition system developed by IBM in the 1990s, which catalyzed interest in automated processing of handwritten text for postal systems globally.

In parallel, the finance industry began leveraging machine learning for credit scoring and fraud detection, utilizing algorithms to sift through immense transaction datasets to identify anomalies and predict client creditworthiness. These initial strides laid the groundwork for widespread adoption and adaptation across varied sectors.

3.1.5 Machine Learning as the Bedrock of Advanced AI Systems

The interdependence between machine learning and advanced AI is profound. Machine learning algorithms underpin the decision-making processes of AI systems, enabling them to learn, adapt, and predict with high accuracy. AI systems capitalize on machine learning's ability to process and analyze data efficiently, driving innovation in fields such as natural language processing, autonomous systems, and predictive maintenance.

The collaboration of AI systems with machine learning is particularly evident in healthcare, where predictive models assess patient data to forecast disease progression and recommend treatment pathways. In the automotive industry, machine learning informs autonomous vehicle systems, enhancing navigation and collision avoidance through real-time decision-making.

The synergy between machine learning and AI is forecasted to continue evolving, with machine learning incrementally enriching AI's capacity to deliver intelligent services and solutions, bridging theoretical exploration with practical deployment.

3.1.6 Real-World Case Study: Transforming Retail with Machine Learning

To illustrate the real-world application of machine learning, consider the retail sector, which has harnessed its power to redefine customer experiences and optimize supply chains. A prime example is Amazon, which utilizes machine learning algorithms for product recommendation engines that personalize shopping experiences based on individual buying behaviors.

Amazon's recommendation system predicts customer preferences by analyzing patterns in browsing history and past purchases, a practice that significantly increases customer engagement and sales. Moreover, machine learning optimizes logistics by forecasting demand and streamlining inventory management, reducing operational costs while ensuring product availability.

This practical application exemplifies how machine learning transforms data into actionable strategies that drive business value and consumer satisfaction. By infusing technology with customer-centric insights, organizations can harness the vast potential of machine learning to foster growth and innovation.

The subsequent section will delve into demystifying neural networks, elucidating how these systems inspire and enhance machine learning's capabilities through bio-inspired models that echo the complexities of human cognitive processes.

Demystifying Neural Networks

In the intricate architecture of artificial intelligence, neural networks stand as one of its most profound innovations. These complex structures, inspired by the biological neural networks of the human brain, are pivotal in enabling machines to perform tasks that once seemed insurmountable. As we embark on this journey to demystify neural networks, we begin by exploring the foundational layers that form the core of these systems: input, hidden, and output layers. Understanding these layers is crucial to unraveling the sophistication behind neural network tasks, such as image recognition and voice synthesis.

The basic unit of a neural network is the neuron, a computational model inspired by the neurons in our brains. Each artificial neuron receives input, processes it, and emits an output. These neurons are organized into layers, each playing a specific role. The input layer is where raw data enters the network. This could be pixel data from an image, sound waves from a recording, or any other form of sensory data. The processed information then passes through one or more hidden layers, where the actual magic of transformation and learning happens. Each neuron in these layers applies a weighted transformation to input signals, followed by a non-linear activation function, allowing the network to learn complex patterns and representations. Finally, the manipulated data reaches the output layer, which produces the network's final prediction or decision.

Understanding the flow of data through these layers is essential in grasping how neural networks can learn to perform specific tasks. The organization into layers allows neural networks to break down complex problems, which parallels the hierarchical processing evident in the human brain. For instance, during image recognition, the initial layers might detect edges, while deeper layers identify more intricate features like shapes and objects, culminating in a comprehensive understanding of the image itself.

One of the pivotal advances in neural networks is deep learning, a subset of machine learning, where networks comprise many hidden layers, vastly enhancing their capabilities. Deep learning enables these systems to perform tasks with unprecedented accuracy by processing vast amounts of data through a model's hierarchical structure. The concept of backpropagation plays a crucial role in this process. It is a method used to calculate the gradient of the loss function with respect to each weight by the chain rule, allowing the model to learn and adjust weights effectively. This method fine-tunes the network's learning by minimizing error rates, steering the network closer to optimal predictions.

For example, consider the process of training a deep learning model to recognize cats in images. Initially, the network might confuse cats with similar animals due to a lack of clear context. Here, backpropagation adjusts the weights of the connections based on the degree of error in recognition, gradually refining the network's ability to differentiate a cat from similar imagery over numerous iterations.

To translate this into a practical scenario, let's explore self-driving cars, an application benefiting immensely from neural networks. These vehicles rely on convolutional neural networks (CNNs), a specialized kind of neural network particularly effective at processing pixel data. CNNs empower self-driving cars to interpret a continuous stream of visual data captured by cameras; they identify objects such as pedestrians, street signs, and other vehicles, ensuring safe navigation. The inherent ability of neural networks to classify and make sense of complex patterns in real-time exemplifies their transformative potential in creating intelligent systems capable of learning independently from their environment.

Moreover, neural networks play a significant role in voice synthesis technologies, such as speech recognition and text-to-speech systems. By leveraging recurrent neural networks (RNNs), which are especially adept at handling sequential data, these systems can process and understand spoken language, providing immediate feedback and responses. Take, for instance, digital assistants like Siri or Alexa. They harness the power of RNNs to not only recognize and interpret user commands but also to engage conversationally, improving with continued use through continuous learning mechanisms.

Yet, understanding neural networks is not solely about examining individual applications. It's about recognizing their potential to revolutionize how we interact with technology, imparting machines with a degree of understanding and perception mirroring human cognition. Real-world instances, such as predictive text input or recommendation systems on platforms like Netflix, illustrate how neural networks subtly integrate into our everyday technology, enhancing user experience by crafting suggestions based on learned patterns.

A case study exemplifying the transformative power of neural networks can be seen in the healthcare industry. IBM's Watson leverages neural networks to assist doctors by diagnosing diseases. By analyzing a broad spectrum of medical records and imaging data, Watson can suggest potential diagnoses and treatment plans with a level of accuracy that rivals trained medical professionals. This integration underscores a collaborative future where AI complements human expertise, augmenting decision-making capabilities in critical sectors.

As we deepen our exploration into the applicability of these systems, it becomes evident that neural networks are not just a technological novelty but a transformative tool poised to unlock new horizons of digital innovation. In the ensuing sections, we will venture further into the role of data processing in AI, illuminating how datasets serve as the lifeblood that fuels the neural networks and other AI models, bridging the theoretical concepts of neural architectures with tangible technological advancement.

The Power of Data Processing

In the vast landscape of artificial intelligence, data stands as both the canvas and the palette from which art is created. Machine learning algorithms, irrespective of their sophistication, rely fundamentally on data to learn, evolve, and adapt. This subchapter delves into the substantial role of data processing in AI, exploring how data is collected, managed, and analyzed to empower AI systems and illustrating why effective data handling is essential for transforming theoretical AI models into practical applications.

The Backbone of AI: Understanding Data's Role

Data might be termed as the 'new oil' in the modern digital economy. However, unlike crude oil, which holds intrinsic value as a raw material, data's worth is realized primarily through processing. In its raw form, data can be likened to unrefined resources: vast, disorganized, and often noisome. The first transformative step in any AI endeavor is turning this raw data into something structured, clean, and insightful. This transformation involves a meticulous process of collecting, cleaning, and preprocessing data before it even enters the machine learning pipelines that power artificial intelligence.

Data Collection: Gathering the Essentials

The data lifecycle begins with its collection, a task requiring precision and strategic planning. Different sectors utilize varying methods to gather data, tailored to each industry's needs. In healthcare, for example, electronic health records and medical imaging databases provide an enormous wealth of information. In contrast, the retail sector leverages customer interactions, transaction histories, and social media feedback to analyze purchasing behaviors.

One cutting-edge example of data collection is in the field of autonomous vehicles. These vehicles are equipped with a myriad of sensors, including LiDAR, cameras, and GPS systems, to collect real-time data about their surroundings. This amassed data serves to train machine learning models to assist in navigation, obstacle detection, and decision-making processes. In this setting, effective data collection is not only foundational to development but also critical to operational safety and reliability.

Cleaning and Preprocessing: The Art of Refinement

Once data is gathered, it must undergo purification—a process known as data cleaning and preprocessing. This stage is critical in shaping raw data into a structured, logical format ready for computational analysis. Data cleaning involves the removal of inaccuracies, duplication, and corruptions that could skew machine learning models. Cleaning techniques include handling missing values, correcting inconsistencies, and eliminating outliers that do not align with general patterns.

Preprocessing extends beyond mere cleaning, introducing broader tasks such as normalization and transformation. Normalization is crucial in ensuring that disparate data attributes are brought to a uniform scale, preventing features with large numerical ranges from disproportionately impacting model training. Meanwhile, transformation processes convert data into formats more conducive to analysis, such as converting categorical variables into numerical ones through encoding techniques.

Innovations in the financial industry illustrate the power of preprocessing. Here, historical transaction data is meticulously curated through feature engineering—constructing meaningful input features from raw datasets. This process might involve time-series transformations or sentiment analysis on textual data, optimizing input quality and helping predictive models achieve sophisticated levels of accuracy in risk assessment and fraud detection.

The Ethics of Data Collection and Management

While data collection powers innovation, it simultaneously raises ethical considerations, particularly concerning data privacy and security. The influx of personal data necessitates stringent regulatory compliance and ethical guidelines to protect individual rights. Regulations like the General Data Protection Regulation (GDPR) put forth stringent data protection measures, ensuring transparency and granting users control over their data.

A case in point can be observed in the healthcare industry, where data sensitivity is paramount. The deployment of AI in personalized medicine demands robust anonymization techniques, encrypting patient information without sacrificing analytical precision. Similarly, implementing differential privacy—a technique that adds noise to datasets—can prevent individual data traceability while preserving dataset accuracy.

The Challenges and Rewards of Big Data

Big data technologies present a paradigm shift in processing capabilities, facilitating the analysis of extensive and complex datasets beyond the reach of traditional processing tools. The shift to distributed computing platforms, such as Hadoop and Spark, revolutionizes data handling by offering scalable solutions for managing and processing voluminous data with efficiency.

In the field of e-commerce, big data analytics unlocks extensive consumer insights. Retailers harness clickstream data, product usage statistics, and customer feedback to fine-tune marketing strategies, thus personalizing user experiences and enhancing customer loyalty. Big data's potential to shape commercial profitability exemplifies its power to convert theoretical models into impactful business mechanisms.

However, with benefits come challenges. The growing volume and velocity of data necessitate advanced storage solutions and data governance strategies. Maintaining data integrity while ensuring swift retrieval and real-time processing adds layers of complexity, demanding specialized infrastructure and expertise.

Practical Application: A Case Study in Healthcare Data Utilization

Consider a hospital system leveraging big data analytics to improve operational efficiency and patient care outcomes. By integrating data from electronic health records, imaging databases, and IoT-enabled devices monitoring vital signs, the hospital creates a comprehensive health analytics platform. This system predicts patient admissions and optimizes resource allocation, reducing operational costs and wait times.

Moreover, the system identifies high-risk patients, enabling proactive interventions and personalized treatment plans. Data-driven insights from genomic data and treatment histories empower clinicians to adopt predictive models for disease progression, thereby enhancing preventive care and reducing readmission rates.

By leveraging robust data processing platforms, this system provides a testament to the transformative potential of data in healthcare—improving care quality, patient experience, and institutional efficiency. As readers journey into the next subchapter, they will gain insights into algorithmic craftsmanship, learning how specific AI techniques translate processed data into actionable intelligence, further bridging the gap between digital theory and practical implementation.

Algorithmic Craftsmanship

In the world of artificial intelligence, algorithms are the unseen architects meticulously designing the bridges between raw data and actionable insights. Much like a master craftsman at work, algorithm developers construct these mathematical frameworks with precision and foresight, understanding that their designs will significantly influence the performance and efficacy of AI systems. As we delve into the essence of algorithmic craftsmanship, it becomes evident that choosing the right algorithm can be the difference between a functional AI solution and an exceptional one.

Craftsmanship in Algorithm Design

Designing algorithms is an art rooted in both complexity and simplicity. At its heart, it requires a deep understanding of diverse problem spaces and a judicious application of mathematical principles. The process of algorithm development starts with defining clear objectives - what specific task should the AI accomplish? Once the goal is clear, developers must select or create an algorithm that not only meets the task's requirements but also operates efficiently within the parameters of speed, accuracy, and resource consumption.

Take, for example, the development of algorithms in natural language processing (NLP). Here, the challenge often lies in devising methods that can effectively parse and interpret the nuances of human language. Algorithms that excel in this domain must meticulously understand and process context, semantics, and syntax, transforming unstructured text into structured data that AI can exploit. The celebrated BERT (Bidirectional Encoder Representations from Transformers) algorithm is a prime example of this intricate craftsmanship. By pre-training deep bidirectional representations by jointly conditioning on both left and right context in all layers, BERT represents a paradigm shift in how machines understand language.

Core Algorithm Types and Their Applications

One cannot overstate the diversity of algorithms present in the AI landscape, each tailored for a specific purpose and condition. Here, we explore some pivotal algorithm types that have cemented their positions in the AI toolkit:

1. Decision Trees: Resembling a flowchart, decision trees are intuitive and natural for human understanding. They are particularly potent at classification and regression problems, making decisions based on data points until a desired outcome is reached. Decision trees excel in situations where data can be cleanly segmented and where model interpretability is valuable. For instance, in finance, they are often used for credit scoring and risk assessment due to their clear and logical decision-making process.

2. Support Vector Machines (SVM): SVMs are robust classifiers and regressor algorithms that work by finding a hyperplane in an N-dimensional space (N being the number of features) that distinctly classifies the data points. They are particularly effective in high-dimensional spaces and are well-suited for text classification tasks. For example, SVMs have been widely used in identifying spam emails, significantly improving the accuracy and reliability of filtering mechanisms.

3. Clustering Algorithms: These algorithms, including k-means and hierarchical clustering, group sets of objects in such a way that objects in the same group (or cluster) are more similar to each other than to those in other groups. Clustering is instrumental in market segmentation, image compression, etc. A notable application of clustering is in customer segmentation for marketing campaigns, where understanding distinct customer groups can lead to targeted and effective marketing strategies.

4. Neural Networks and Deep Learning: While neural networks might have already been discussed in earlier subchapters, it is the algorithms used within these networks that warrant attention. Algorithms like Convolutional Neural Networks (CNNs) are specialized for image processing and recognition tasks. On the other hand, Generative Adversarial Networks (GANs) have opened new horizons in creating images, music, and art, often indistinguishable from those created by humans.

The Selection Process: Art and Science

Choosing the right algorithm is not merely a technical decision; it's an art form that marries data science with domain expertise. It requires an intricately balanced consideration of the algorithm's strengths, limitations, and the nuances of the problem domain. Factors like data volume, feature dimensionality, and the complexity of the relationships between data elements often govern the algorithm selection process.

Practical Scenario: In the healthcare industry, developing systems to predict patient outcomes often involves handling a myriad of complex datasets with numerous variables, from genetic markers to lifestyle data. Here, the algorithm selection process might favor decision trees and SVMs for their interpretability and ability to handle nonlinear relationships, providing healthcare professionals with actionable insights they can trust.

Optimizing Algorithms for Performance

After selecting the appropriate algorithm, the journey doesn't end there. Fine-tuning is critical, ensuring that the algorithm yields the best performance. Hyperparameter tuning, for instance, plays a pivotal role across many algorithms, defining how learning occurs. Techniques such as grid search and random search are employed to identify the optimal hyperparameter settings, improving both accuracy and efficiency.

Optimizing an algorithm often involves iterative testing and enhancement. For example, in a cybersecurity application tasked with identifying potential threats through network traffic analysis, it might begin with a basic clustering approach. Over time, as the system encounters diverse data patterns, developers might incorporate reinforcement learning strategies to evolve the algorithm, enhancing its efficacy in threat detection and prediction.

Real-World Application: Algorithmic Craftsmanship in Action

To illustrate how algorithmic craftsmanship is applied effectively, we'll explore a case study from e-commerce - optimizing recommendation systems. Recommendation systems have become ubiquitous, not just enhancing user experience but also significantly boosting sales and customer satisfaction.

Case Study: Amazon's Recommendation Algorithm

Amazon, one of the world's largest e-commerce platforms, leverages advanced algorithms to provide personalized product recommendations to its users. The system uses a blend of collaborative filtering, content-based filtering, and deep learning to analyze user behavior, purchase history, and product preferences.

By examining patterns across millions of users and products, the algorithms predict what a customer might be interested in next. This approach relies on algorithmic craftsmanship, constantly refining and testing their models to improve accuracy and relevance. The result is a dynamic recommendation system that seamlessly integrates into the user shopping experience, driving engagement, and sales through personalized touchpoints.

This powerful example of algorithmic craftsmanship underscores the importance of thoughtful algorithm selection and refinement, illustrating how these efforts translate to tangible business outcomes. In doing so, it highlights the need for continuous innovation as AI systems assimilate more diverse and large datasets, paving the path for even more sophisticated AI solutions.

As we transition to the next subchapter, which will focus on bridging these theoretical concepts with real-world application, we need to bear in mind that while algorithms form the backbone of AI technology, integrating these into functional systems requires a broader strategic approach. By understanding and mastering the art of algorithmic craftsmanship, we can unlock AI's full potential, setting the stage for its transformative impact across industries.

Bridging Theory with Application

In the ever-evolving landscape of artificial intelligence, theoretical understanding is only the starting point of a transformative journey. The real value of AI materializes when these theoretical constructs seamlessly transition into practical, real-world applications that reshape industries and enhance human potential. This subchapter serves as a bridge, navigating the reader from the intricate worlds of machine learning algorithms and neural networks into vivid demonstrations of

AI's impact. It navigates through dynamic terrains, showcasing how AI's building blocks translate into actionable solutions across diverse sectors like finance, healthcare, logistics, and more.

AI in Finance: Powering Precision and Fraud Detection

The financial industry, characterized by vast quantities of data and the criticality of accuracy, finds itself at the forefront of AI innovation. Artificial intelligence in finance is indispensable for tasks that require precision and rapid decision-making, such as fraud detection, credit scoring, and investment strategies.

Consider the example of JPMorgan Chase, which has actively integrated AI into its operations with a program known as COiN or Contract Intelligence. This AI-driven system is proficient in reviewing legal documents and extracting critical information, a task that would traditionally consume thousands of employee hours. COiN's ability to sift through legal contracts and identify important data points not only increases efficiency but also reduces the potential for human error.

In fraud detection, AI models excel by analyzing patterns and identifying anomalies in transaction data. Machine learning algorithms are tailored to parse through historical transaction data, learning from established fraud patterns to flag suspicious activities in real-time. This predictive capability is essential in maintaining the integrity of financial transactions, protecting consumers and corporations from potential threats.

Healthcare Revolution: From Diagnosis to Treatment

The integration of AI in healthcare has great promise, driven by the potent combination of data accessibility and advances in analytical techniques. AI's potential to analyze complex datasets transforms the landscape of patient care, ranging from diagnosis to personalized treatment plans.

One notable instance is with IBM's Watson Health, which

employs AI to assist oncologists. This AI system reviews extensive medical literature and patient data to suggest tailored treatment options for cancer patients. By analyzing thousands of research papers and clinical trials in a fraction of the time it would take a human, Watson provides insights into potential treatment paths based on the latest research findings, thus becoming an invaluable tool in empowering doctors with information-rich decision-making.

Moreover, AI facilitates the development of more precise diagnostic tools. Algorithm-driven imaging systems are now capable of detecting conditions such as diabetic retinopathy and even certain cancers at an earlier stage than traditional methods. This early detection capability is pivotal in initiating timely and potentially life-saving treatments.

Logistics and Supply Chain Optimization

In the logistics and supply chain sector, the application of AI fosters enhanced operational efficiency and improved customer satisfaction. By employing machine learning algorithms, companies can predict demand more accurately, optimize delivery routes, and manage inventory effectively.

Amazon, a quintessential example of AI application in logistics, employs sophisticated algorithms for its fulfillment processes. The company's AI systems analyze massive datasets of customer orders, supplier schedules, and shipment routes to optimize warehouse stocking and delivery planning. This optimizes the balance between supply and demand, ensuring that the right products are available at the right time and location, minimizing lead times and fostering client satisfaction.

AI-powered predictive analytics tools also play a significant role in anticipatory logistics, enabling companies to foresee potential supply chain disruptions and conflicts. This proactive approach allows businesses to devise contingency plans and maintain uninterrupted services, crucial for fostering resilient supply chains in an increasingly globalized world.

Realizing AI Potential: A Case Study Approach

The theoretical underpinnings laid out in earlier subchapters manifest distinctively when viewed through the lens of practical application. Let's delve into a specific case illustrating AI's transformative power within an industry: the application of AI in predictive maintenance within the manufacturing sector.

Case Study: Siemens and Predictive Maintenance

Siemens, a global giant in industrial engineering, offers an exemplary case of AI's role in predictive maintenance. By leveraging AI technologies, Siemens has significantly improved the maintenance processes of its industrial machinery, yielding substantial cost savings and productivity enhancements.

Traditionally, maintenance of industrial equipment has been reactionary. Machines are repaired post-failure, a process that can lead to costly downtimes and operational inefficiencies. In contrast, predicted maintenance uses AI algorithms to preemptively identify machinery parts that might fail, allowing for timely interventions.

Siemens employs an AI-driven system that continuously monitors sensor data from its machines. This real-time analysis enables the system to detect subtle patterns indicating wear and tear, deviations from standard operation, or impending failures. The AI models are trained over vast historical datasets, refining their precision in identifying anomalous behaviors. Such predictive insights facilitate pre-scheduled maintenance activities, drastically reducing downtime and enhancing productivity.

The shift to predictive maintenance, powered by AI, simplifies the complex decision-making process regarding when and how to maintain equipment. Simultaneously, it prevents costly emergency repairs and extends the lifespan of machinery components.

Driving Forward: The Road to Future Applications

As we stand at the cusp of the next frontier in digital transformation, the synergies between AI's theoretical frameworks and their practical implementations will continue to proliferate. Each building block discussed throughout this chapter – whether rooted in machine learning, neural networks, data processing, or algorithmic design – sets the groundwork for innovative solutions yet to unfold.

Artificial intelligence, driven by these foundational technologies, holds the promise of continually transforming industries, elevating human capabilities, and redefining the boundaries of what is achievable. As readers transition to the subsequent chapters, it is these tangible applications, grounded in robust theoretical foundations, that empower them to envisage and harness AI's full potential in an ever-evolving technological landscape.

As we conclude Chapter 3, "Building Blocks — The Technology Behind AI," it is critical to recognize the foundational elements that lay the groundwork for understanding artificial intelligence. We have journeyed from the rudimentary principles of machine learning—the driving force behind AI's ability to discern patterns in multifaceted data sets—to the intricate world of neural networks, where AI emulates human cognitive processes to tackle complex tasks. In exploring the pivotal role data plays in advancing technological frontiers, we have uncovered the vast potential that lies in efficient data processing and management, essential for translating theoretical concepts into actionable insights.

The art of algorithmic craftsmanship has further amplified our appreciation for selecting the right tools to navigate specific AI challenges, optimally tailoring solutions to diverse contexts. Finally, the seamless bridging of theory with real-world application exemplifies the transformative power of AI across various industries, paving the way for innovation that drives meaningful change.

In reflecting on these key components, it becomes evident that the confluence of machine learning, data processing, and algorithmic precision is not merely academic but a catalyst for practical evolution. I encourage you to integrate these insights into your own personal and professional arenas, leveraging the immense potential AI holds to redefine solutions and create new opportunities.

As we proceed to the next chapter, expect to delve deeper into the tangible applications of AI across sectors, exploring how these building blocks culminate in technologies that reshape our world. Embark on this journey with an open mind and a renewed eagerness to harness the synergy of AI and human ingenuity for a future brimming with possibilities.

CHAPTER 4: HEALTHCARE REVOLUTION - AI'S IMPACT ON MEDICINE

In an age where technological advancement seems to outpace human imagination, the marriage of artificial intelligence and medicine heralds a new dawn in healthcare. This chapter, Healthcare Revolution — AI's Impact on Medicine, invites you to explore how AI is reshaping everything from diagnostics to patient care with unprecedented efficiency and accuracy.

Imagine a world where the detection of diseases occurs the moment they manifest, where treatments are as unique as the individual receiving them, and where healthcare operations run with the precision of a finely tuned machine. This is not the distant future; it is the emerging reality made possible through AI's integration into the medical field. Our journey begins with examining how AI transforms diagnostics, a critical first step in the healthcare continuum. From the intricate images produced in radiology to the rhythmic complexities of cardiology, AI offers precision and speed that surpass human capacity, enabling earlier disease detection and significantly improving patient outcomes.

The revolution extends beyond diagnostics; it permeates personalized patient care. Increasingly, treatments are being precisely tailored to the genetic and medical profiles of individuals, moving away from one-size-fits-all therapies. AI algorithms evaluate massive datasets to craft personalized treatment plans, predicting drug responses and identifying optimal care paths. Through these technological advancements, we discover healthcare that not only treats but anticipates patient needs.

AI also emerges as a supportive ally in decision-making for healthcare professionals. As we will explore, it supplements the clinical judgment of practitioners by offering evidence-based recommendations drawn from exhaustive analysis of current research and guidelines. Yet, the narrative of progress urges us to balance the digital with the human, ensuring AI enhances rather than replaces the empathetic touch that defines effective medical care.

Our exploration then shifts from patient care enhancement to the internal mechanisms of healthcare facilities. AI optimizes administrative and logistical operations, allowing healthcare workers to dedicate more time to patient care. As AI streamlines everything from patient record management to predicting hospital admission rates, it frees up resources, enabling healthcare systems to function more efficiently and effectively.

However, it would be remiss to paint this revolution without acknowledging the challenges that accompany it. Integration of AI into healthcare systems is not without its barriers—data privacy concerns, the necessity for algorithmic transparency, and the imperative of cross-disciplinary collaboration all demand our attention. Addressing these challenges is crucial for establishing robust ethical frameworks and governance structures, ensuring AI's responsible application in healthcare environments.

As we delve into these thematic areas, each subchapter will unfold the layers of AI's transformative impact on medicine, illustrating not only the potential it holds but also the accountable path we must navigate. Join me as we explore the dynamic interplay between technology and medicine, setting the stage for a new era of healthcare that champions collaboration between human intelligence and artificial acumen.

Transforming Diagnostics — Precision and Speed

Artificial Intelligence (AI) stands on the precipice of redefining how diagnostic medicine operates, transcending traditional methodologies and ushering in a future where precision and speed are paramount. In this subchapter, we delve into the transformative power of AI in medical diagnostics, demonstrating how it is reshaping the landscape of healthcare by enabling quicker, more accurate, and often cheaper means of identifying diseases.

AI's potential to revolutionize diagnostics is primarily anchored in its ability to process and analyze large volumes of data far more efficiently than the human mind. At the core of this transformation is machine learning, a subset of AI that utilizes algorithms to identify patterns and predict outcomes. In fields such as radiology and cardiology, AI assists in scrutinizing medical imaging to uncover findings that may escape human detection. This chapter will explore how this technology enhances diagnostic accuracy and speed, ultimately leading to earlier disease detection and improved patient outcomes.

To understand the impact of AI in diagnostics, it is crucial to examine the healthcare industry's existing challenges and limitations. Traditional diagnostic methods, while effective in many instances, often rely heavily on the skill level and subjective interpretation of individual healthcare professionals. This approach can result in variability and sometimes delays in diagnosis, particularly in complex cases. AI seeks to mitigate these issues by providing consistent, data-driven analysis that complements human expertise.

AI-Enhanced Radiology

In radiology, AI systems analyze medical images such as X-rays, MRIs, and CT scans to detect anomalies with increased precision. By using deep learning algorithms trained on thousands of images, AI can identify patterns indicative of specific conditions, such as tumors or fractures, often with greater speed and accuracy than a human radiologist. This technology reduces the burden on radiologists and minimizes the risk of oversight. For instance, Google's DeepMind Health has collaborated with several hospitals, including Moorfields Eye Hospital in London, to develop AI algorithms that can detect eye diseases from retinal scans. These collaborations are proving that AI can reliably assist in diagnosing conditions like diabetic retinopathy and age-related macular degeneration, often in real-time and with high precision.

Another practical example is IBM's Watson, which has been deployed in various hospitals to assist in interpreting cardiology imaging results. By integrating historical data from numerous patients, the AI system can offer insights into heart conditions, providing diagnostic suggestions that help cardiologists make timely and informed decisions.

Speed and Early Detection

AI not only amplifies the precision of diagnostics but also revolutionizes their speed. Fast processing of imaging and data allows for significantly shorter turnaround times. In emergency situations, where time is a critical factor, AI's ability to deliver immediate diagnostic insights can mean the difference between life and death. A study conducted by Stanford University demonstrated that their AI algorithm is capable of matching the performance of radiologists in diagnosing pneumonia from chest X-rays, often processing the same data in a fraction of the time.

This ability to provide quick, accurate diagnostics extends beyond imaging. AI's role in laboratory testing and pathology is set to expand. Algorithms have been developed to analyze blood samples and biopsy slides to identify cancerous cells more quickly and accurately than human pathologists. Inflammation markers, infection indicators, and genetic mutations relevant to numerous conditions are also within the interpretive reach of advanced AI systems. The opportunity to detect diseases at an earlier stage holds immense potential for improving patient prognoses and extending lives.

AI in Cardiovascular Diagnostics

Cardiovascular diseases remain a leading cause of mortality worldwide, underscoring a significant need for advancements in this area. AI is redefining cardiovascular diagnostics through innovations such as wearable technology and remote monitoring systems, which continuously collect data about a patient's heart activity. These systems feed data into AI algorithms that detect irregular heart rhythms, predict the likelihood of cardiac events, and alert healthcare providers of potential issues before they become emergencies.

Consider a study from the Mayo Clinic, where researchers demonstrated how an AI approach to interpreting electrocardiograms (ECGs) predicted the onset of atrial fibrillation, a condition typically difficult to diagnose, by learning patterns in the initial data that could point to future development of the condition. This capability of early detection aligns with proactive patient management strategies, allowing for interventions that can prevent the worsening of the disease.

Real-Life Applications and Case Studies

The integration of AI in diagnostics is not merely theoretical. Many healthcare institutions are already experiencing the benefits. Take the case of Massachusetts General Hospital, where AI is embedded in routine radiology workflows to aid the diagnostic process of various health conditions, including neurological disorders and musculoskeletal injuries. The AI's predictions assist decisions related to further testing and treatments, proving its worth as an integral support system in medical practice.

In another case, a cohort study conducted across several medical centers implementing AI-driven diagnostics showed a noticeable improvement in the turnaround times for serious conditions like stroke, where time-critical decisions can vastly alter patient outcomes. Stroke assessment, primarily based on time-sensitive CT or MRI scans, has gained new efficiency through AI capabilities, which enable clinicians to focus on intervention strategies rather than analysis.

Navigating the Future

As we advance, the role of AI in transforming diagnostics will likely expand into more interactive and patient-centered applications. We anticipate personalized diagnostic pathways and more transparent AI systems that build trust among healthcare professionals and patients alike. The continuous expansion of AI's diagnostic capabilities paves the way for an integrated healthcare system where technology and human expertise work in tandem, optimizing patient outcomes and propelling the medical field into an era defined by precision, speed, and a relentless pursuit of innovation.

In the subsequent subchapter, we will explore how AI's ability to interpret individual patient data fosters the development of personalized treatment plans, a natural progression from AI-enhanced diagnostics to tailored patient care strategies. The shift toward personalization in healthcare promises not only enhanced treatment efficacy but also a paradigm in which patients feel seen and understood by the technology supporting their care.

Personalized Treatment Plans
— Tailoring Care with AI

In the ever-evolving landscape of modern medicine, artificial intelligence presents a transformative force, most visibly in the realm of personalized treatment plans. As healthcare continues to shift towards a patient-centered approach, AI plays a pivotal role in tailoring care to the individual needs of each patient. By deciphering complex genetic information, assessing comprehensive medical histories, and considering environmental factors, AI systems are pioneering an era of bespoke healthcare strategies that promise to enhance efficacy and outcomes significantly.

The concept of personalized medicine is predicated on the nuanced understanding that each patient's physiological and genetic identity is unique. Traditional, one-size-fits-all treatment protocols often fail to address the complex interplay of factors influencing individual health responses. Enter AI, with its capacity to analyze voluminous datasets at high speed, identifying patterns and insights that can be leveraged to craft targeted therapeutic strategies. This approach stands in stark contrast to the generalized treatment models of the past, offering the potential for unprecedented levels of precision.

At the heart of personalized treatment is the integration of genetic data. The Human Genome Project, completed in 2003, laid the foundation for our understanding of human genetics; yet, translating this information into practical medical applications remained a bottleneck—until AI entered the scene. AI algorithms can swiftly process vast arrays of genomic data, flagging specific genetic markers indicative of particular health risks or conditions. For instance, researchers have developed AI models capable of predicting cancer susceptibility by analyzing patient genomes and comparing them against large datasets to find risk-related mutants or variations.

Beyond genetics, AI enhances personalized healthcare by synthesizing comprehensive medical histories with real-time health data. Consider diabetes management: traditionally, patients receive standard medication advice based on population averages. However, an AI-driven approach can assess individual blood sugar trends, dietary habits, and lifestyle choices, adjusting treatment recommendations dynamically to each individual's needs. This level of personalization not only improves disease management but also empowers patients, giving them a deeper understanding and control over their health.

Another significant AI application lies in pharmacogenomics— the study of how genes affect a person's response to drugs. AI's capability to predict drug responses can help mitigate the trial-and-error nature of prescribing medications, thus reducing adverse effects and ensuring efficacy. For instance, some patients metabolize drugs like warfarin (a common anticoagulant) too quickly or too slowly due to genetic differences, affecting dosage requirements. AI models can analyze genetic profiles to anticipate these variances, allowing physicians to prescribe the right dose from the outset, minimizing the risk of complications like bleeding or clotting.

A testament to AI's potential in personalized treatment is exemplified by the partnership between IBM Watson Health and Memorial Sloan Kettering Cancer Center in New York. Together, they have developed an AI system trained on thousands of cases to recommend personalized cancer treatment plans. By analyzing patient records alongside medical literature, the system suggests treatment options that oncologists might otherwise overlook, potentially improving survival rates and quality of life for cancer patients. This collaboration has set a precedent for how AI can transform cancer care, epitomizing healthcare's shift towards precision.

One of the most compelling advantages of AI in personalized medicine is its ability to adapt and refine treatment plans over time. Through machine learning, systems continuously improve as they amass experiences and outcomes from prior cases. This iterative learning process ensures that treatment strategies are not only data-driven but dynamically evolving, based on clinical feedback and new research. AI's rapidly increasing knowledge base allows it to identify and predict trends before they fully manifest, offering proactive rather than reactive healthcare.

AI's implementation extends to chronic and progressive diseases, where ongoing management is crucial. Consider rheumatoid arthritis, a debilitating autoimmune disorder that varies significantly between patients in terms of symptoms and severity. AI systems can track the progression of the disease through patient-reported outcomes and regular diagnostic results, adjusting treatment protocols to align with each patient's evolving condition. Such adaptable strategies can lead to better-managed symptoms, reduced side effects, and improved overall patient well-being.

Despite its potential, integrating AI into personalized care requires thoughtful consideration of ethical and practical challenges. Ensuring data privacy is paramount, as the personalized approach relies on extensive access to sensitive personal data. Additionally, the black-box nature of some AI models—where the decision-making process is not transparent —poses challenges in aligning AI recommendations with the regulatory standards that demand accountability. Successfully overcoming these obstacles is critical for fostering trust in AI-driven personalization and ensuring its equitable and responsible deployment in healthcare.

A practical application of AI in personalized treatment can be illustrated through the story of Genomics Medicine Ireland (GMI), a company that leverages AI to develop personalized medicine strategies by collecting genetic information from thousands of volunteers. This initiative aims to identify correlations between genetic traits and various health conditions, such as rare diseases, thus devising precise treatments. Let us consider patient Sarah, who was diagnosed with a rare genetic disorder. Traditional treatments had limited effects and led to multiple complications. Through GMI's personalized approach, Sarah's genomic data was analyzed, identifying a genetic variant that predisposed her to an atypical response to standard medication. Using AI-driven insights, doctors adjusted her treatment plan, introducing medications tailored to her genetic profile, which successfully stabilized her condition and significantly improved her quality of life.

As we further explore the capabilities of AI in medicine, we transition towards understanding AI not just as a tool for personalization but as an active collaborator in the clinical decision-making process, where its potential as a supportive partner enhances healthcare professionals' expertise. Through evidence-based recommendations and integration into day-to-day medical practices, AI emerges as a crucial ally in refining the delivery of care, ultimately ensuring the best possible patient outcomes in an increasingly complex healthcare ecosystem.

Augmenting Clinical Decision-Making — AI as a Supportive Partner

In the rapidly evolving domain of healthcare, clinical decision-making remains a cornerstone of effective patient treatment.

The complexity lies not only in the vast array of available medical information but also in the dynamic nature of each patient's unique condition. This is where artificial intelligence steps in, transforming how decisions are made by augmenting the capabilities of healthcare professionals. In this subchapter, we delve into the multifaceted role of AI in supporting clinical decisions, highlighting its potential to enhance, rather than replace, human expertise.

Historically, clinical decision-making relied heavily on the knowledge and experience accumulated by physicians over years of practice. However, the increasing amount of medical data, coupled with the pace of new medical research, challenges even the most seasoned professionals to stay updated. AI systems are uniquely positioned to bridge this gap by processing voluminous datasets, distilling critical information, and providing evidence-based recommendations. By digesting the latest research, clinical guidelines, and patient data, AI algorithms can assist healthcare providers in developing more comprehensive and precise treatment plans.

Consider the AI-driven platforms that are now being integrated into emergency rooms and intensive care units. These systems analyze patient vitals in real-time and cross-reference them against historical patient data and global clinical studies. Such capabilities enable physicians to detect abnormalities or potential complications more swiftly. For instance, an AI system might alert a physician to an unnoticed pattern of declining blood pressure and heart rate, enabling early intervention and potentially preventing a life-threatening event.

Another area where AI demonstrates its value is in the realm of predictive analytics. By utilizing machine learning models, healthcare providers can forecast patient outcomes based on an array of factors such as genetics, lifestyle, and past medical history. This predictive capability is vital for chronic disease management, where an understanding of potential future complications can guide preventative care strategies. Tailored alerts generated by AI systems can remind clinicians about preventive measures such as screenings or lifestyle recommendations that are most appropriate for individual patients.

Moreover, AI augments clinical decisions by synthesizing a clinician's intuition with algorithmic precision to deliver holistic care. A platform like IBM Watson Health exemplifies this integration, providing oncologists with treatment recommendations based on comprehensive literature reviews and case studies from around the world. This synthesis offers a second layer of scrutiny and validation for critical decisions, reassuring patients and healthcare providers alike that the chosen therapeutic path is both innovative and grounded in evidence.

However, while AI enhances clinical judgment, it is imperative to maintain the human touch and ensure that machine-generated insights are interpreted within the context of personal and patient-centered care. Physicians possess the nuanced understanding of patient needs and societal norms that AI algorithms may not fully grasp. An example of this is the differentiation of care required for terminal patients, where the decision-making process demands sensitivity to patient preferences, family dynamics, and cultural considerations—elements that require empathy and human interaction.

To illustrate AI's supportive role in clinical settings, let's explore a real-life case study from the Mayo Clinic, where integration of an AI platform has notably improved the treatment protocol for sepsis. Sepsis, a life-threatening response to infection, requires prompt diagnosis and intervention. By utilizing an AI model trained on vast datasets encompassing medical history, biomarkers, and previous case studies, clinicians at Mayo Clinic have reduced the time to diagnosis and treatment initiation. This AI system continuously monitors patient data, identifying subtle signs of deterioration before they manifest in severe symptoms. The proactive alerts have not only improved patient outcomes but also streamlined workflow efficiency by enabling the healthcare team to prioritize their attention to those in critical need.

As AI continues to evolve, its role in clinical decision-making will expand, offering even more sophisticated tools to enhance patient care. Yet, the successful implementation of these technologies hinges on ensuring they are used to complement—rather than replace—the vital human element of medicine. This partnership between human expertise and artificial intelligence promises to revolutionize the quality and effectiveness of healthcare delivery, paving the way for a future where clinicians can navigate the complexities of medical care with unprecedented clarity and confidence.

Transitioning from the supportive role of AI in clinical decision-making, we now turn our attention to its impact on healthcare operations. While patient care remains the ultimate focus, optimizing the operational aspects of healthcare facilities is crucial in creating a system that is both efficient and effective. In the next subchapter, we explore how AI is reshaping healthcare operations, unlocking new levels of management efficiency that allow healthcare facilities to provide better care with fewer resources.

Enhancing Healthcare Operations
— Efficiency in Management

In the bustling landscape of modern healthcare, the deployment of artificial intelligence (AI) technologies is not limited to the confines of patient diagnostics and treatment plans. This subchapter sheds light on how AI is fundamentally reconfiguring healthcare operations, bringing a new frontier of efficiency and precision to the management sphere. Through task automation and data-driven insights, AI not only increases the efficacy of healthcare systems but also enables medical institutions to focus more on providing quality care. As we unravel the potentials of AI in this domain, the narrative will be anchored by relatable scenarios and real-world case studies that underscore the transformative power of this technology.

Contemporary healthcare systems are often bogged down by administrative burdens, inefficiencies in logistics, and limitations in resource allocation. The ramifications include longer patient wait times, increased operational costs, and a reduced focus on patient-centered care. AI's prowess lies in its ability to streamline these processes, engendering a seamless workflow that enhances the operational dynamics of hospitals and clinics.

One of the most significant advantages of AI in healthcare operations is in automating routine and repetitive tasks. Administrative duties such as scheduling appointments, processing insurance claims, and maintaining patient records are crucial yet time-consuming. Intelligent systems equipped with natural language processing (NLP) and machine learning algorithms are adept at handling these tasks with speed and precision. For instance, AI platforms like Olive are revolutionizing the way hospitals process paperwork, reducing the administrative load on human staff and cutting down on errors that are common in manual data entry.

A critical function of AI in optimizing healthcare operations lies in the management of patient records and data storage. Traditional paper records and even some digital systems are often plagued by inefficiencies, where data retrieval can be tedious and prone to human error. AI-driven electronic health records (EHR) systems are designed to mitigate these issues. By embedding AI into EHR, healthcare providers can instantly access comprehensive patient information, ensuring that data is not only organized but also easily retrievable. This capability allows medical professionals to quickly review patient histories, allergies, and past treatments, thereby enhancing decision-making processes.

Furthermore, AI's predictive analytics offer a groundbreaking approach to understanding and managing patient flow and resource allocation. By analyzing historical data, AI models can forecast admission rates, predict patient influx in emergency departments, and signal potential staff shortages. This foresight equips hospital managers to make more informed decisions regarding staffing needs, bed availability, and resource management. For example, the Cleveland Clinic has successfully employed AI tools to anticipate patient volumes, which in turn allows them to better distribute staff and resources during peak times, ensuring efficiency and reducing patient wait times.

Another notable application is AI's impact on supply chain logistics within the healthcare industry. Hospitals rely on timely and efficient supply chains to ensure that essential medical equipment, pharmaceuticals, and supplies are available as needed. AI systems facilitate more refined inventory management by accurately predicting demand trends, reducing waste, and minimizing the risk of shortages or overstock situations. Take the case of Stanford Health Care, where AI-driven analytics are used to optimize purchasing patterns, leading to significant savings on procurement costs while maintaining high service levels for patient care.

Moreover, the integration of AI in telemedicine platforms has further extended the operational capacity of healthcare institutions. With the surge in demand for virtual consultations, AI assists in triaging patients, streamlining appointment scheduling, and ensuring a smooth virtual visit experience. This innovation not only extends access to healthcare services but also alleviates pressure on physical facilities, enabling them to focus their resources on critical in-person needs.

To illuminate AI's transformative role in healthcare operations, consider the following case study: In the sprawling metropolis of New York City, Mount Sinai Health System embarked on an ambitious project to revamp its operational framework using AI technology. Faced with rising patient volumes and limited logistical efficiency, the health system turned to AI-driven tools to scrutinize and enhance their operational processes.

By employing AI algorithms, Mount Sinai optimized scheduling systems, significantly reducing patient wait times. The AI systems were designed to analyze historical appointment data, identifying ideal time slots by predicting potential no-show appointments. This allowed staff to overbook intelligently, filling in gaps and increasing overall appointment efficiency. Furthermore, AI was utilized to forecast patient admission patterns, allowing for dynamic resource allocation in emergency departments.

The result was a staggering 20% improvement in appointment availability and a 30% decrease in patient wait times. Additionally, by streamlining patient check-in processes through AI-powered kiosks, the health system saw a reduction in administrative workload, freeing up personnel to engage directly in patient care activities.

As we continue to explore AI's pervasive influence across medical domains, the operational efficiencies garnered through AI underscore its indispensable role in modern healthcare systems. By overcoming existing challenges and reinforcing sustainable practices, AI serves as a catalyst for optimized healthcare delivery, a theme that will inevitably weave itself into our exploration of the subsequent subchapter. The next step in our journey is to address the barriers that must be surmounted to facilitate AI's full adoption and to implement this groundbreaking technology responsibly and ethically across the healthcare sector.

Overcoming Challenges — Barriers to AI Implementation in Healthcare

The healthcare revolution, driven by artificial intelligence, represents a staggering leap forward in the advancement of medical science. However, like any transformative journey, it comes with its own set of hurdles and ethical quandaries. As healthcare systems worldwide embrace AI technologies, they are encountering barriers that necessitate careful navigation and thoughtful solutions to ensure responsible and equitable implementation.

A primary challenge facing healthcare is data privacy. The immense datasets required to train AI algorithms are often sensitive in nature, encompassing personal health information and genetic details. There is an urgent need to address concerns over how this data is collected, stored, and used. The Cambridge Analytica scandal underscored the repercussions of mishandling data privacy. In the context of healthcare, the stakes are even higher because breaches can directly impact patient trust and safety. The General Data Protection Regulation (GDPR), enforced in Europe, represents a step towards safeguarding data privacy by implementing strict guidelines on data usage and user consent. Similarly, the U.S. Health Insurance Portability and Accountability Act (HIPAA) outlines regulations that healthcare institutions must follow to protect patient data. Ensuring compliance with these regulations while using AI systems is crucial for maintaining trust.

In addition to privacy, algorithmic transparency is another barrier in the path of AI integration. AI models, particularly deep learning algorithms, often function as "black boxes" — complex systems whose internal workings are opaque and not easily interpreted by humans. In healthcare, this opacity can lead to hesitancy among practitioners to rely on AI for critical decisions, as understanding the rationale behind the recommendations is essential. For AI to be effective and trusted in medicine, algorithms must be interpretable and transparent. Strides are being made through the development of explainable AI, or XAI, which aims to make AI decision-making processes more understandable to humans. A renowned example is Google's DeepMind, which is working towards creating AI systems capable of explaining their actions to doctors, thereby bridging the gap between machine intelligence and human comprehension.

Cross-disciplinary collaboration is also imperative in overcoming barriers to AI adoption. AI systems in healthcare should not be developed in isolation by technologists alone. Both the tech and healthcare sectors must engage in meaningful dialogue, ensuring that AI solutions are designed with a deep understanding of the clinical environment. This requires fostering partnerships among engineers, data scientists, clinicians, and healthcare administrators. Successful examples of such collaborations include the AI Clinician project by researchers at the Massachusetts Institute of Technology (MIT), where a joint team of computer scientists and clinicians developed a system to improve sepsis management in intensive care units.

Furthermore, there is a need for robust ethical frameworks and governance structures that provide clear guidelines for the deployment of AI technologies in healthcare. These frameworks should address issues such as bias, which can arise from training models on datasets that do not represent the diversity of the population, leading to inaccurate results for marginalized groups. The establishment of committees that review and set ethical standards for AI use in healthcare could provide reassurance to both practitioners and patients.

Education and training are equally vital. Healthcare professionals need to be savvy with AI technologies to optimize their potential while mitigating risks. Medical curricula must incorporate programs that teach both the technical and ethical dimensions of AI. Initiatives, such as the AI for Healthcare Bootcamp organized by Stanford University, offer intensive training for healthcare professionals to bridge the knowledge gap and empower them to use AI tools effectively.

One practical application that illustrates these concepts is the implementation of AI in managing hospital readmissions. The University of Pennsylvania Health System undertook a project that harnessed AI to predict patients at risk of readmission. By using patient data, ranging from socio-economic factors to prior medical conditions, the AI system developed a risk score indicating the probability of readmission. However, to address privacy concerns, they ensured that data collection adhered to strict privacy regulations. They also included clinicians in the algorithm development process to ensure the system was intuitive and aligned with hospital practices, ultimately reducing readmission rates without compromising patient trust.

The journey toward AI integration in healthcare is fraught with complexities. However, by addressing these barriers through ethical guidance, transparent and collaborative approaches, and comprehensive education, the healthcare industry can successfully harness the full potential of AI. As this landscape continues to evolve, the foundation laid today will shape the extent to which AI can revolutionize medicine, prompting us to anticipate future possibilities in the next chapter's exploration of AI's role in other critical sectors.

As we conclude Chapter 4, it is clear that artificial intelligence stands as a transformative force in the realm of healthcare, reshaping diagnostics, treatment plans, and operational efficiencies. We have explored the remarkable capabilities of AI in swiftly analyzing extensive datasets, thereby enhancing the precision and speed of medical diagnostics. Through personalized treatment plans, AI is enabling individualized care strategies that promise improved patient outcomes. Furthermore, AI serves as an indispensable ally in clinical decision-making, aiding healthcare professionals with evidence-based insights while preserving the essential human touch.

Operational efficiency, streamlined by AI's capacity to manage logistical complexities, demonstrates its invaluable contribution beyond patient care, leading to more resource-effective healthcare environments. Yet, as we embrace these advances, we also confront challenges related to ethical implementation and trust. It is imperative that we navigate these complexities with a commitment to responsible AI governance and transparency.

Reflect on how AI's integration into healthcare offers pathways for innovation in your own professional and personal contexts. Whether as a patient, a healthcare professional, or a tech enthusiast, the insights from this chapter highlight how technology can redefine human capabilities within medical fields.

Looking forward, we will transition to explore AI's influence beyond healthcare, delving into its transformative impact across various sectors. As we proceed, consider how the underlying principles of AI's role in healthcare can serve as a foundation for understanding its broader societal implications. Join us as we continue this exploration, reinforcing our collective journey towards a future enriched by symbiotic intelligence.

CHAPTER 5: EDUCATION REIMAGINED — TEACHING AND LEARNING WITH AI

Welcome to an era where the fabric of education is being intricately woven with the threads of artificial intelligence, transforming traditional classrooms into dynamic ecosystems of learning and discovery. In this chapter, we embark on an exploration of how AI is not just supplementing, but fundamentally redefining the ways we teach and learn. As we journey through this landscape, you'll discover how AI-driven tools are reshaping educational experiences, making them more personalized, inclusive, and efficient than ever before.

Education, like technology, is a powerful engine of change that constantly evolves to meet the demands of a rapidly shifting world. Today, as technology advances at an unprecedented pace, the intersection of AI and education promises to revolutionize the learning environment. This chapter delves into AI's profound impact on education, illuminating how it enhances personalized learning experiences, streamlines administrative processes, and opens up new horizons for educators and students alike.

We begin with an exploration of personalized learning, a concept that epitomizes AI's transformative potential in tailoring educational pathways to each learner's unique needs. By leveraging vast data sets, AI tools are capable of customizing content, adjusting difficulty levels, and providing real-time feedback. Through case studies and real-world examples, we unravel how these tools are being effectively implemented to create customized learning experiences that cater to individual student strengths and interests.

Next, we shift our focus to the empowerment of educators, as AI equips teachers with innovative tools to enhance their creative and instructional capabilities. By automating routine tasks and facilitating differentiated instruction, AI enables educators to concentrate more on teaching and engaging with students. The insights provided by AI-driven analytics offer a deeper understanding of student progress, allowing for more informed and tailored pedagogical strategies.

As we continue, we explore how AI is revolutionizing education through automation, streamlining everything from grading to attendance tracking and administrative processes. These automated systems free up valuable time for educators, allowing them to focus more on instruction and less on logistical burdens, thus contributing to a more effective and efficient educational experience.

Inclusivity is another key area where AI is making significant strides, as it creates learning environments accessible to students of diverse needs and backgrounds. By accommodating various learning styles and abilities, AI helps ensure that every learner has the opportunity to succeed, opening doors to educational opportunities that were previously unimaginable.

Finally, we look towards the future, envisioning the opportunities and challenges that lie ahead as AI continues to evolve within the educational landscape. While the potential for innovation is vast, there remain critical considerations regarding data privacy, ethics, and the ongoing need for teacher training. By anticipating and addressing these challenges, we can pave the way for a balanced integration of AI that maximizes its benefits for the generations to come.

As you explore the subsequent sections, it becomes evident that AI's role in education goes beyond mere assistance. It stands as a catalyst accelerating the fusion of human ingenuity and technological prowess. This chapter invites you to envision a future where AI and education exist symbiotically, empowering both educators and learners to achieve unprecedented levels of understanding and insight.

Personalized Learning — Tailoring Education to Each Learner

The dawn of artificial intelligence has ushered in an era of unprecedented opportunity within the realm of education, offering groundbreaking methodologies that can cater to the individual needs of every learner. Personalized learning, supported by AI technology, stands at the forefront of this transformation. By utilizing sophisticated algorithms, AI-driven tools can analyze a student's learning behavior, preferences, and challenges to craft a customized educational journey. This involves the modulation of content delivery, the adjustment of learning pace, and real-time feedback — affording each learner a unique educational experience tailored to suit their individual requirements.

To fully appreciate the transformative power of AI in personalized learning, it is crucial to address how it operates within an educational setting. At its core, AI enables educators and educational platforms to process vast amounts of data that were previously unmanageable. By scrutinizing students' past performance records, interaction patterns, preferences, and learning speeds, AI can predict and suggest the most effective teaching strategies and content for each student. This adaptation goes beyond merely changing the color of an interface or adjusting font size; it deeply personalizes the entirety of a learner's educational experience.

Consider an AI-driven platform deployed in a high school mathematics program. The platform was designed to offer students practice problems and lessons tailored to their current level of understanding. As students progress, the AI monitors their performance, noting which types of problems they consistently solve correctly and which ones they find challenging. This real-time analysis allows the platform to provide problems of appropriate difficulty and targeted hints, ensuring that each student receives assistance precisely where they need it most. Such systems not only help students master the material more effectively but also keep them engaged by providing continuous, appropriately challenging content.

A noteworthy benefit of this approach is its capacity to support the mastery of complex subjects. Traditionally, classrooms have moved at a fixed pace, often leaving some students to struggle or become disengaged. AI-powered tools, however, allow for a mastery-based learning model, where students can only move on to more advanced topics once they demonstrate a strong understanding of current material. This model can be especially beneficial in areas like STEM (Science, Technology, Engineering, and Mathematics), where foundational knowledge is crucial for future success.

One illuminating example of personalized learning in action comes from a study conducted by a leading educational technology company that integrated AI into its language learning app. The app utilized machine learning algorithms to adapt to the learners' language proficiency and learning style. For instance, if a student exhibited difficulty with verbal communication, the app provided additional auditory lessons and exercises focused on speaking and listening. Conversely, students who excelled in reading comprehension received more challenging texts to enhance their vocabulary and understanding. The study reported a significant increase in student engagement and learning outcomes, demonstrating the enhanced efficacy of this tailored approach.

AI-driven personalization goes beyond mere academic improvements; it plays an integral role in boosting learners' confidence and motivation. Students who receive individualized content and support are more likely to experience a sense of accomplishment and empowerment, leading to increased motivation and perseverance. When learners feel that their educational journey is specifically designed for their success, they are more inclined to take ownership of their learning process, resulting in higher rates of success and overall satisfaction.

Moreover, personalized learning can accommodate diverse learning styles and needs, which is critical in today's diverse educational landscape. Traditional educational models often generalize teaching methods, potentially alienating students who do not conform to conventional learning styles. AI tackles this issue by adjusting content and instructional approaches to cater to visual, auditory, and kinesthetic learners alike. By offering a range of learning experiences — from interactive simulations and visualizations to audiobooks and gamified lessons — AI ensures that all students, regardless of their predominant learning style, can access and benefit from tailored educational experiences.

The integration of AI into personalized learning also holds particular promise for students with learning disabilities or those requiring special accommodations. AI's ability to adapt and personalize education can make learning more inclusive. Tools equipped with AI can offer various levels of support to different learners, such as text-to-speech features for students with dyslexia or adjustable syntax complexity for students with autism. By providing customized tools and resources, AI helps remove barriers that have historically excluded these learners, offering them a fair opportunity to succeed alongside their peers.

However, while AI's capabilities in personalizing education are vast, they come with a set of challenges that cannot be overlooked. One of the primary concerns is the reliance on accurate data. The effectiveness of AI tools and platforms hinges on the availability and quality of data collected from each learner. Educators and institutions must ensure that data collection is comprehensive and ethical, safeguarding students' privacy while providing the necessary insights required for AI systems to function effectively.

Another challenge is the need for educational content that is compatible with AI platforms. Traditional curricula may need reformulations to fit AI's adaptive framework, requiring investments in content development and teacher training. Educators must also be trained to interpret data and insights generated by AI tools, transforming them into actionable educational strategies. Schools and educators must prioritize skills development, ensuring that they are equipped to leverage AI technologies effectively and enhance learning experiences.

Despite these challenges, the potential gains of AI-driven personalized learning in improving educational outcomes are nothing short of revolutionary. Real-life applications of this technology have already begun to manifest globally, reshaping how education is delivered and received. Such advancements are set to continue impacting educational paradigms, contributing to a more adaptive and inclusive learning environment.

In practice, consider a suburban school district that adopted an AI-powered platform to tailor math instruction. The district's objective was to bolster student performance in standardized state exams. Through using an adaptive system that assessed and responded to individual student performance in real-time, the platform offered practice problems and tutorials tailored specifically to each student's learning gaps and strengths. Within a year, the school district witnessed an impressive increase in math proficiency scores, with students reporting greater confidence and less anxiety about exams. This case study exemplifies how AI-driven personalization can simultaneously address individual learning needs and achieve broader educational objectives.

As we transition to the next topic, we shift our focus from the profound impact AI has on student learning to how it supports and empowers educators. By streamlining administrative tasks and enhancing instructional capabilities, AI not only transforms educational outcomes for students but also elevates the teaching profession itself.

Empowering Educators — The AI Advantage

As the educational landscape continuously evolves, educators are increasingly challenged with balancing the demands of administrative tasks, curriculum development, and direct engagement with students. Fortunately, AI has emerged as a transformative ally, offering unprecedented opportunities to enhance the teaching experience and empower educators in meaningful ways. This subchapter explores the profound impact of AI on education from an educator's perspective, delving into the ways AI can streamline administrative duties, facilitate differentiated instruction, and provide valuable insights into student progress. By doing so, AI allows teachers to focus on their primary passion: teaching and enriching the lives of their students.

AI Streamlining Administrative Tasks

Administrative duties, though crucial, often consume a significant amount of an educator's time and energy. From record-keeping to scheduling, these tasks can detract from a teacher's ability to engage with students and deliver impactful lessons. AI technologies are changing this paradigm by offering tools that streamline administrative processes, thus allowing educators to dedicate more time to pedagogy.

For instance, AI-powered platforms such as GradeScope and Turnitin are revolutionizing the grading process. GradeScope uses AI to assist educators in grading assignments across a variety of subjects, providing consistent feedback and reducing grading time by up to 89 percent. This system allows teachers not only to validate student submissions quickly but also to identify areas where students might struggle, enabling more targeted interventions. Similarly, Turnitin, best known for its plagiarism detection, utilizes AI to provide feedback on written content, analyzing grammar, structure, and originality and offering constructive cues for improvement.

In scheduling, tools like Otter.ai are integrating AI technology to transcribe lectures and meetings, creating searchable and shareable notes, which can be invaluable for educators managing large classes or involved in numerous committee meetings. These AI solutions enhance an educator's efficiency, allowing for greater focus on direct student interaction and curriculum development.

Designing Differentiated Instruction with AI

One of the cornerstones of effective education is the ability to cater to a diverse range of learning needs, and AI offers innovative solutions in this respect. Differentiated instruction, tailored to accommodate different learning styles and paces, becomes more attainable with AI's support.

AI-driven platforms such as Carnegie Learning's MATHia and NoRedInk provide personalized learning experiences by adapting content to individual students' proficiency levels and learning speeds. MATHia, for example, uses predictive analytics to examine student responses and tailor future content based on their performance, ensuring they face neither too much challenge nor too little. This allows students to construct a solid understanding of mathematical concepts at their own pace. On the language arts front, NoRedInk offers adaptive writing exercises that adjust to student interests and skill levels. By engaging students with relatable and relevant content, these platforms enhance engagement and comprehension.

Furthermore, AI can assist teachers in identifying student learning preferences and difficulties. Platforms like Coursera and Khan Academy integrate AI to analyze learner behavior and suggest teaching interventions. By interpreting data on engagement patterns and learning progression, these platforms empower educators to customize instructions, thus enhancing student engagement and learning outcomes.

Gaining Insights into Student Progress

The ability to gain actionable insights into student progress is invaluable for educators seeking to maximize the impact of their teaching. AI provides tools that allow teachers to assess student understanding in real time, facilitating prompt and effective intervention where necessary.

Tools such as Edmodo and ClassCraft utilize AI to track and analyze student performance data. Edmodo, for example, offers educators a dashboard that highlights student engagement, performance trends, and areas needing improvement. By mapping a student's journey through the curriculum, these platforms inform teachers about aspects that may require more focused attention.

ClassCraft takes a gamified approach, using AI to monitor student behavior and motivation. By assigning 'experience points' for participation and collaboration, the platform promotes positive behavior and academic engagement, providing educators with a creative method to maintain a dynamic and motivated classroom environment.

AI-driven learning analytics also plays a crucial role in the early identification of at-risk students. Predictive modeling tools can flag patterns of disengagement or declining performance, alerting educators to students who may need additional support. By catching these issues early, teachers can implement targeted interventions to guide students back on track.

Real-Life Case Study: The AI Advantage in Action

A compelling example of AI's empowering potential for educators can be seen in the implementation of Smart Sparrow's adaptive learning platform at Arizona State University. Smart Sparrow enabled instructors to create "adaptive lessons" using AI algorithms that dynamically adjusted content based on student interactions. This approach not only improved student engagement and understanding but also provided educators with detailed analytics on student performance and learning behaviors.

In one course, biology instructors utilized Smart Sparrow to address common misconceptions in genetics. As students progressed through the course, the platform adapted lesson difficulty based on individual students' comprehension levels. Educators received regular performance reports that identified trends and problem areas, allowing them to adjust teaching strategies in real time. The outcome was remarkable: student pass rates increased by 24 percent, and instructors were able to offer more personalized feedback during office hours and class discussions.

Such transformative examples underscore the practicality and effectiveness of incorporating AI into educational practices. By empowering educators through administrative efficiencies, differentiated instruction, and actionable insights, AI not only enhances the teaching experience but also leads to improved student outcomes. As we transition to the next subchapter, we will examine how AI's transformative power extends beyond individual classrooms to reshape educational systems through automation, enhancing overall efficiency and accuracy.

Automated Systems — Efficiency in Education

In the rapidly changing world of education, efficiency stands as a cornerstone to maximizing both instructional and learning potential. By introducing advanced automation through artificial intelligence, educational systems can seamlessly transition toward enhanced efficiency, liberating teachers and students from the shackles of mundane tasks. This subchapter delves into the significant ways AI-driven automated systems are revolutionizing the educational infrastructure, with both small-scale impacts in the classroom and broad-scale effects across institutions.

Automating Grading Systems

One of the initial inroads AI has made into education is in the realm of automated grading systems. Traditionally, teachers have invested significant time in grading assignments, quizzes, and tests—a time-consuming endeavor that often detracts from more interactive and pedagogical engagements with students. AI-empowered grading tools have transformed this landscape, introducing accuracy and expedience in assessing student work.

Consider the real-world application of AI in grading platforms such as "Gradescope" and "Turnitin." Gradescope, in particular, uses AI to assist educators in grading assignments quickly and consistently. By employing machine learning algorithms, it categorizes common student errors and assigns grades in a uniform manner. Not only does this save time, but it also ensures fairness by reducing human bias and error. This efficiency allows educators to dedicate more time to curriculum development and individualized student support, enhancing the overall educational experience.

Streamlining Attendance Tracking

Another domain where AI automation is proving transformative is attendance tracking. In traditional settings, recording attendance is a routine affair often fraught with errors and inefficiencies. AI now offers robust solutions that streamline this process, ensuring greater accuracy with less teacher intervention.

AI-driven systems employing facial recognition technology are at the forefront of this evolution. Schools across Asia, for instance, have successfully implemented facial recognition and biometric systems to automatically log student attendance. This technology identifies students in real time as they enter the classroom, logging their presence much more accurately than conventional methods. An example of this is found in certain universities in China, where AI recognition systems are used not only for attendance but also for alerting teachers about students who are frequently tardy or absent. The automation of this task frees educators and administrative staff from manually handling attendance, allowing them to focus on more directly impactful educational duties.

Enhancing Administrative Processes

Beyond grading and attendance, AI's automation capabilities extend into administrative processes that fundamentally underpin educational institutions. Tasks such as scheduling, resource allocation, and communication channels are experiencing significant improvements due to AI integration.

For example, chatbots are becoming increasingly common in handling routine administrative inquiries, both from students and parents. Educational institutions like Georgia State University have implemented AI-driven chatbots named 'Pounce' to mitigate the volume of student queries related to enrollment, financial aid, and course details. These bots are designed to offer instant responses, improving response times while reducing the workload of administrative staff. The efficiencies gained through such systems enhance the operational capabilities of educational institutions, providing smoother communication and organization-centric processes.

AI in Resource Allocation

When it comes to resource allocation, AI's analytical tools process large sets of data to optimize usage and distribution of resources. AI platforms can analyze student enrollment trends, capacity of classrooms, and faculty workload to suggest optimal scheduling fits and course distributions.

A pertinent case is the deployment of AI algorithms by the Los Angeles Unified School District (LAUSD), which serves one of the largest student populations in the United States. By using AI to analyze data sets related to classroom usage, student demographics, and financial constraints, LAUSD has optimized its resource distribution, ensuring appropriate teacher-to-student ratios and timely availability of educational materials. This data-driven approach ensures that educational resources are allocated efficiently and equitably, addressing the diverse needs of the student body.

Increasing Pedagogical Focus

By automating routine tasks, AI also allows educators to refocus their efforts on pedagogy and student interaction. Tools like AI-based lesson planning systems provide educators with dynamic content suggestions and formative assessment indicators, tailoring these to each classroom's unique context.

For instance, "Smart Sparrow" offers a personalized learning design platform that aids teachers in crafting and delivering adaptive lessons. By employing data analytics, this platform suggests educational resources and methods that might be most effective given the specific needs of a teacher's class. Teachers can then focus on engaging with students directly, enhancing interactive learning experiences and fostering deeper educational connections.

Practical Application: A Case Study in the United Kingdom

A shining example of AI-powered automation in practice is the "City of London School," a UK-based institution that implemented an AI platform designed to handle administrative and pedagogical tasks. This platform, named "CrossKnowledge," automates scheduling, assists in career assessment, and provides a robust database for lesson planning and student engagement follow-ups. This has significantly reduced administrative burdens, enabling teachers to enhance their focus on teaching innovations and student interactions, showcasing how AI automation can be harnessed to elevate overall educational quality.

The extensive adoption of AI in the City of London School illustrates the profound impact that efficient, automated systems can have on education. By integrating AI into routine chores, the school not only improves efficiency but also boosts the capacity for innovation in teaching methods, allowing educators to concentrate on creating transformative learning experiences.

As this subchapter underscores, the potential of AI-driven automated systems is vast, offering the promise of increased efficiency, accuracy, and effectiveness in the education sector. By freeing educators from time-intensive administrative duties, these systems empower them to return to the heart of education —teaching and engaging with their students.

This exploration of how AI automation elevates educational efficiency seamlessly transitions into the next subchapter, which delves into AI's pivotal role in fostering inclusive learning environments, ensuring no student is left behind in the era of educational transformation.

Fostering an Inclusive Learning Environment

The promise of a truly inclusive educational system has long been the aspiration of educators and technologists alike. In this pursuit, artificial intelligence offers groundbreaking opportunities to create environments where every learner, regardless of their background or learning ability, can thrive. This subchapter delves into how AI technologies assist in breaking down traditional barriers to education, foster diversity in learning, and promote equitable access for all students.

Breaking Down Barriers

In a conventional classroom setting, uniformity often prevails, and this can unintentionally marginalize students who do not fit the standard mold due to differing learning abilities or disabilities. AI has the potential to effectively dismantle these barriers by enabling customized educational experiences. For example, adaptive learning platforms, powered by AI, continually assess a student's progress and adapt content and strategies to meet their unique learning styles. This capacity to dynamically tailor educational experiences ensures that all students, including those with disabilities, have a personalized path that aligns with their individual needs.

Consider the example of students with dyslexia. Traditional text-heavy educational content might pose significant challenges for them. However, AI-driven tools such as text-to-speech applications can transform text into audio, providing a much-needed alternative medium for understanding classroom material. These tools can be further enhanced by natural language processing capabilities that allow for seamless integration and real-time adjustments to learning content, catering to students' evolving comprehension levels.

Facilitating Language Diversity

Language should never be a barrier to education. AI's ability to process and understand human languages has revolutionized how diverse classrooms manage linguistic challenges. For instance, AI-based translation tools can render classroom instructions and texts into multiple languages in real-time, ensuring that language differences do not hinder a student's ability to learn. Such technology has become particularly useful in multilingual schools and learning institutions, allowing non-native speakers to receive and participate in education on an equal footing with their peers.

An inspiring case is the use of real-time translation devices in a school district serving a high percentage of immigrant families. By employing AI to translate teachers' spoken words instantly into students' native languages, these schools have significantly reduced the language gap. Students who previously struggled to keep up due to language barriers are now actively engaged in learning activities, contributing to an inclusive and harmonious learning environment.

Enhancing Support for Students with Special Needs

AI holds immense potential for supporting students with special needs, facilitating their integration into mainstream education. AI applications can identify early signs of learning disabilities through the analysis of data patterns over time. For example, by monitoring students' interactions with educational software, AI can detect when a student is struggling with specific types of problems, prompting timely interventions. This early detection allows educators and parents to initiate support mechanisms sooner, improving educational outcomes for these students.

One practical application is seen with AI-driven applications in addressing autism. These tools can analyze social interaction patterns, often lacking in autistic children, and propose activities that help these children develop the necessary social skills in safe, controlled environments. Moreover, AI personal assistants, programmed with empathetic and adaptive algorithms, can provide on-demand support to autistic students, guiding them through challenging tasks or social interactions that they might find overwhelming.

Promotion of Diverse Learning Styles

Every student learns differently, and a one-size-fits-all approach often falls short of realizing each individual's potential. AI technology can be pivotal in recognizing and accommodating diverse learning styles. By leveraging machine learning algorithms, educational platforms can classify students based on their preferred learning methodologies—be it visual, auditory, or kinesthetic—and adapt content delivery to match these preferences.

In a classroom utilizing such technology, a student identified as a visual learner receiving instruction on a complex science concept might be offered interactive diagrams and video content, rather than textual descriptions and lectures. Another student who favors an auditory style would receive the same content through podcasts or specialized audio tutorials.

Real-World Applications and Success Stories

The practical application of AI in creating inclusive educational settings is well-documented through numerous success stories across the globe. One notable instance is the Smart School initiative implemented in Finland, which employs AI to support diverse student populations, fostering inclusivity and enhancing learning outcomes. In these schools, AI tools autonomously tailor lessons to meet individual student needs, accommodating different learning abilities, mitigating language barriers, and supporting special needs students. The initiative reports improvements not only in academic achievements but also in student self-esteem and collaboration among students with varying needs.

Another compelling case is the collaboration between Google and a non-profit educational organization to develop AI tools aimed at assisting visually impaired students. The project focuses on building smart classroom environments where AI interprets written material, oral instructions, and even captures visual cues in video feed to provide context and descriptions, allowing visually impaired students to engage fully in class activities.

Integrating AI with Human Support

While AI is a powerful tool for inclusion, its most effective applications occur when it works alongside human educators. Teachers play a crucial role in interpreting AI insights and directing interventions in a manner that promotes empathy and understanding, traits that AI is still learning to master. By working in tandem, AI can handle data-driven tasks and automate modifications while educators maintain the human connection that inspires learning.

As AI continues to evolve and its capabilities expand, the potential for fostering a truly inclusive educational landscape grows. The future holds the promise of classrooms where every student, regardless of their unique learning needs, sees themselves represented and supported in their educational journey.

By transitioning into the next section, which explores the future of AI in education, we will delve into the opportunities and challenges that such advancements present. How can we ensure that the benefits of AI are equitably distributed, and what measures need to be in place to safeguard privacy and ethical standards? These considerations are crucial as we anticipate and navigate the evolving role of AI in education.

Let's examine a practical example of inclusivity through AI. A pilot program in San Diego employs AI to support students with varying physical disabilities. This initiative pairs AI-powered devices, tailored to each student's mobility limitations, to facilitate better engagement with coursework, peer collaboration, and teacher interaction. Initial results show a marked increase in academic participation and performance among students who were previously disconnected from traditional educational formats. This example underscores AI's transformative potential in realizing inclusive, effective education for every student, paving the way for continuous exploration into advanced AI applications within educational systems.

The Future of AI in Education — Opportunities and Challenges

The landscape of education is fertile ground for innovation, and as we look towards the future, the role of artificial intelligence in education presents both unprecedented opportunities and formidable challenges. By transcending traditional boundaries of time and space in learning environments, AI promises to revolutionize how we approach teaching and learning in myriad ways. At the same time, it introduces unique challenges that educators, technologists, policymakers, and students must collaboratively navigate. In this subchapter, we delve into these dynamics, considering the innovations on the horizon and the obstacles that must be overcome to harness AI's full potential in education.

Opportunities on the Horizon

AI stands as a catalyst, primed to elevate educational experiences to new heights. As technology evolves at an exponential rate, several key opportunities emerge:

1. Ubiquitous Learning Environments: The future of education may well be distinguished by its fluidity, wherein learning can happen anywhere and at any time, facilitated by AI. Imagine a world where virtual AI tutors in your mobile device can accompany students throughout their daily lives, offering instant support and insights as needed. These AI systems can track student progress continuously, adjusting content dynamically to suit the learner's context and mood.

2. Advanced Data Analytics: The increasing sophistication of AI-powered data analytics will enable institutions to gather and interpret vast amounts of educational data swiftly. This data will not only inform day-to-day instructional decisions but also long-term strategic planning. Universities and schools will be able to predict trends, allocate resources more effectively, and tailor curricula to upcoming societal needs.

3. Interdisciplinary Learning: AI will pave the way for a truly interdisciplinary approach to education. With the ability to process and synthesize information from diverse fields rapidly, AI can provide students with a more integrated and holistic learning experience. This empowers students to tackle complex, real-world problems that require multifaceted thinking, from climate change to global health.

4. Virtual and Augmented Reality: AI-enhanced virtual and augmented reality platforms will bring immersive learning experiences closer to reality. Students will be able to explore historical events, simulate scientific experiments, or even collaborate in a digital ecosystem with peers worldwide—transforming theoretical knowledge into practical application.

5. Customized Educational Content: As AI systems become more adept at processing natural language, they can generate educational materials that align precisely with a student's learning objectives and style. This means textbooks, assignments, and assessments may soon be automatically created, tailored to the unique needs of each cohort.

Challenges Along the Path

With these promise-laden opportunities come significant challenges. Each hurdle presents complex questions that require careful consideration and strategic action:

1. Ethical and Privacy Concerns: As AI systems collect and analyze personal data on an unprecedented scale, issues related to privacy and data security will come to the fore. While the insights derived from student data are invaluable, the potential for misuse or unethical exploitation of this information necessitates robust ethical guidelines and regulatory frameworks.

2. Bias and Fairness: AI systems, if left unchecked, can perpetuate existing biases present in their training data. It is crucial to ensure that educational AI applications are developed inclusively, representing diverse perspectives, and continuously audited to prevent discrimination against any student group.

3. Teacher Training and Adaptation: Introducing AI technologies into the classroom requires educators to become adept at integrating these tools into their teaching practices. This will demand comprehensive professional development programs designed to help teachers and administrators adapt to this new educational paradigm.

4. Access and Equity: To truly transform education on a global scale, AI-driven educational resources must be accessible to learners from all walks of life. This involves addressing the digital divide and ensuring that students in underserved areas

have both the infrastructure and support necessary to benefit fully from AI-enhanced learning.

5. Managing Technological Change: The rapid pace of technological innovation can outstrip educational institutions' ability to adapt. Balancing the need for cutting-edge technology with the enduring educational structures requires strategic vision and nimbleness.

A Glimpse into Future Learning: Case Study - Smart Classrooms in Action

Consider the case study of a progressive educational project in an urban school district in Singapore, where a collaboration between tech companies and educational authorities has birthed the vision of a "Smart Classroom." In this environment, AI plays a pivotal role in facilitating learning and administrative processes.

Each classroom is equipped with AI-powered systems that monitor and analyze student engagement in real-time through a combination of sensors and cameras. Utilizing advanced computer vision techniques, these systems can gauge the level of understanding based on students' facial expressions and interactions. As a result, teachers receive immediate feedback, allowing them to adjust their instructional strategies on the fly.

Moreover, the AI system integrates with adaptive learning platforms that customize instructional materials in real-time. If a student appears to struggle with a particular concept, the system automatically suggests additional resources or alters the teaching approach to one that better suits the student's learning style.

On the administrative side, routine tasks such as grading and attendance are managed by the system, freeing teachers to focus more on interactive and nuanced aspects of teaching. Importantly, ethical guidelines and data protection measures are rigorously enforced, prioritizing the student's privacy and ensuring the usage of AI remains transparent and beneficial.

The implementation of these smart classrooms has shown promising results, evidencing increases in student engagement and comprehension. This initiative serves as a testament to the potential of AI to create responsive and dynamic educational environments where both human and artificial intelligence empower and enhance the learning experience.

Transitioning towards the conclusion of our broader examination of AI in education, it is imperative to view these technological strides not as isolated innovations but as interconnected elements of a robust educational ecosystem. As we navigate these evolving landscapes, we must ensure the principles of equity, ethics, and inclusivity remain at the forefront, guiding the integration of AI in a manner that truly serves every learner.

As we conclude our exploration of AI's transformative role in education, it's clear that we stand at the precipice of a new era where learning is more personalized, inclusive, and efficient than ever before. Through AI-driven tools, we are witnessing education molded around each student's unique needs, empowering educators to focus more on fostering genuine connections and creative pedagogies. Automation liberates valuable time and resources, allowing both students and teachers to concentrate on achieving educational excellence.

Moreover, AI's ability to break down barriers ensures that all learners, regardless of their background or abilities, have the opportunity to flourish. This chapter highlighted the profound impact of AI in creating a learning environment that celebrates diversity and inclusivity, ensuring equitable access for all.

Yet, as we move forward with these advancements, we must remain vigilant about the accompanying challenges, such as data privacy and ethical considerations. By addressing these issues head-on and investing in continuous teacher training, we ensure that the integration of AI is not only successful but sustainable.

As we turn our gaze to the upcoming chapter, we will delve deeper into how AI continues to redefine professional industries beyond education. With a focus on real-world applications, the next segment of our journey will explore how we can harness artificial intelligence to navigate and transform business landscapes. By understanding and applying these insights, you are encouraged to not only embrace but lead in this digital revolution, positioning yourself and your organization as pioneers in an AI-empowered world.

Harness these insights and venture forward, equipped with the knowledge to thrive in a future where human and artificial intelligence collaborate to achieve unprecedented innovations and successes.

CHAPTER 6: CREATIVITY UNLEASHED: THE ARTS MEET AI

I n the constantly evolving dance between human innovation and technological advancement, creativity stands as a testament to our unparalleled capacity for imagination and expression. Yet, in this era of rapid digital transformation, even the bastions of artistic endeavor find themselves at a crossroads as they encounter a formidable partner: artificial intelligence. This chapter, Creativity Unleashed: The Arts Meet AI, offers readers a profound exploration of AI's burgeoning influence within the artistic realm, challenging traditional paradigms and inviting us to reconsider what constitutes creativity and collaboration.

The convergence of the arts and artificial intelligence is neither a sudden revolution nor an accidental collision but rather a carefully woven tapestry with roots tracing back to the early experiments that first saw technology sidling into artists' studios. In our opening subchapter, The Genesis of AI in the Creative Arts, we trace the origins of this intersection and illuminate the path that led AI from curious novelty to indispensable tool. By delving into these historical milestones, we not only appreciate the gradual acceptance of AI's role in shaping new artistic languages but also lay the groundwork for understanding its present-day capabilities.

As AI evolves, it has transcended its role as a mere tool to become a muse, a source of inspiration that reshapes the way artists conceive and create. In the section titled AI as a Muse — Redefining Artistic Inspiration, we delve into the groundbreaking ways AI has invigorated the creative process. Through vivid examples from music, visual arts, and literature, readers will witness the symbiotic relationship where artists engage with AI not in adversarial terms, but as co-collaborators in expanding the horizons of what is artistically possible.

To fully grasp AI's transformative potential in the arts, it is imperative to explore its practical applications. Our journey through the arsenal of AI-driven artist tools reveals the tangible ways in which algorithms, software, and platforms are revolutionizing creative workflows. In the subchapter Practical Applications — Tools of the AI-Driven Artist, case studies illuminate how artists leverage AI to refine their crafts and bring their creative aspirations to fruition with unprecedented precision.

Yet, as technology and humanity's creative spirit merge, questions arise about originality, authorship, and the very nature of creativity. In Collaboration and Critique — Human Creativity in the Age of Intelligent Machines, we confront these tensions head-on by examining successful artist-AI collaborations alongside critical perspectives. Here, ethical debates provide a profound backdrop against which readers are invited to ponder the nuanced dynamics of this new era of artistic partnership.

Finally, we cast our eyes to the horizon with Imagining the

Future — AI's Expanding Horizon in the Arts. By envisioning a future where AI's capabilities integrate seamlessly with human creativity, we extend an invitation to dream of infinite artistic possibilities yet to be realized. This section propels readers to contemplate how AI might not only enhance but also redefine the boundaries of art as we know it.

Creativity Unleashed: The Arts Meet AI serves as a compass guiding readers through this transformative landscape, setting the stage for broader discussions on AI's societal impact and inspiring a deeper exploration of how technology might redefine not just art, but the essence of human ingenuity itself.

The Genesis of AI in the Creative Arts

The technological dawn of artificial intelligence in the creative arts marks one of the most fascinating intersections of human ingenuity and machine innovation. As we delve into the genesis of AI's role within the creative domain, we illuminate the historical pathways that have carved out a space for digital intelligence in artistry, evolving from primitive computational systems to sophisticated creative collaborators. To understand the transformative journey AI has embarked upon in reimagining artistic landscapes, we must first trace its origins and growth within the artistic sphere.

The Birth of Tech-Art Convergence

AI's introduction to the creative arts can be traced back to the explorative efforts in the mid-20th century. Alan Turing, whose pioneering work in computing laid the groundwork for artificial intelligence, once mused on the potential for computers to create art, foreshadowing a digital revolution in creative disciplines. Early computational creativity was experimental, often led by computer scientists with an artistic inclination. These trailblazers explored the capabilities of nascent digital systems to create visual and auditory works, setting the stage for a symbiotic relationship between technology and art.

In the 1960s, the first notable attempts to integrate computer science with art emerged. This period saw artists like Frieder Nake and Harold Cohen begin to create algorithmically generated art. Cohen's AARON, an AI program designed to generate original drawings, became one of the earliest examples of computers used in art creation. AARON signified the beginnings of a new creative tool, one that artistically inclined not only the technophiles of the world but the artists themselves. These endeavors were met with a skeptical reception from the traditional art world, yet they laid the necessary groundwork for future exploration.

Pioneering Projects and Early Innovators

The gradual evolution of AI within the creative arts is marked by several key projects and innovators who expanded the horizons of how art could be conceived and produced. In the 1980s, David Cope developed EMI (Experiments in Musical Intelligence), a program capable of composing music in the style of famous composers like Bach and Mozart. Cope's work opened the doors for AI-generated music, showcasing how algorithms could grasp the intricacies of musical composition and raise questions about creativity and originality.

The late 20th and early 21st centuries witnessed the acceleration of AI tools for artistic purposes, spurred by advancements in machine learning and neural networks. With these developments, AI capabilities evolved from rudimentary line drawings and music compositions to complex, nuanced creations, including photorealistic art and symphonies that challenged traditional boundaries. One notable experiment in the late 1990s was the introduction of DeepDream by Alexander Mordvintsev, a computer vision program developed by Google that uses a convolutional neural network to find and enhance patterns in images, often resulting in fantastical and psychedelic visuals.

The Emergence of AI in Visual Arts

Visual arts have particularly benefited from AI developments, encompassing everything from digital imaging to animation. Artists adopted AI to create portraits, landscapes, and abstract art which pushed the boundaries of perception. AI-driven tools like Photoshop's AI-based neural filters allowed even greater innovation in the manipulation and editing of visual content, giving artists new brushes and canvases to explore their creativity.

The rise of generative adversarial networks (GANs) has further fueled innovation in this space. GANs, developed by Ian Goodfellow and his colleagues in 2014, have the capability to generate new, never-before-seen images indistinguishable from genuine photographs. Notable artworks, such as "Portrait of Edmond de Belamy" created by the Paris-based collective Obvious using GANs, sold at a Christie's auction for $432,500, exemplifying AI's capacity to create art that holds value and intrigue in the traditional art market.

From Skepticism to Acceptance

The initial skepticism that surrounded AI's endeavors in the arts has gradually shifted towards acceptance and even enthusiasm in many circles. The transformation of AI from a perceived threat to artistic authenticity to a recognized tool for creative assistance underscores the adaptability of artists and technologists alike. As AI continues to mature and refine its creative outputs, the conversation increasingly centers on how rather than if AI belongs in the realm of the arts.

This shift in perception was catalyzed by AI's evolution from producing mere novelties to shaping compelling, emotionally resonant works. AI can assist in overcoming creative blocks or generating ideas, thus extending an artist's creative reach. AI-powered platforms such as OpenAI's ChatGPT and DALL-E have facilitated unprecedented opportunities for collaborative creativity, highlighting AI's potential as a co-creator rather than a usurper of human artistry.

Practical Application and Case Study: The Case of AI-Generated Art Installations

One practical application demonstrating the transformative power of AI in the arts is its role in modern art installations. In 2018, TeamLab, an interdisciplinary art collective, harnessed AI to produce immersive digital environments. These spaces, like the "MORI Building Digital Art Museum: teamLab Borderless" in Tokyo, blend art, science, and technology, epitomizing the convergence of AI and creativity.

The museum features rooms with interactive digital displays that continuously evolve in response to visitors' movements and interactions. AI algorithms process input from sensors, adapting the visual and auditory elements in real time. This experience demonstrates AI's capacity to create dynamic, mutable art forms that transcend traditional static expressions, highlighting the limitless potential for AI to transform spaces and experiences.

In these installations, AI does more than assist; it becomes a medium, suggesting that the future of art may lie not just in the hands of individuals, but in the collaborative efforts between artists and intelligent systems. This partnership yields art that is living, responsive, and imbued with the potential for continuous transformation—a concept compelling audiences to reconsider the definitions of both art and artist.

As we transition to the next subchapter, we delve deeper into how AI not only aids creativity but acts as a source of inspiration, redefining the essence of artistic muse. The following segment explores AI as an instigator of innovation, inviting artists to push the boundaries of their expressive potential while working harmoniously with their digital counterparts.

AI as a Muse — Redefining Artistic Inspiration

In the rich tapestry of artistic expression, inspiration has often been a mysterious force, a guiding hand that elevates the mundane into the extraordinary. From the muses of Greek mythology, who were believed to bestow creativity upon mortals, to nature's endless wonders that have inspired countless masterpieces, the wellspring of artistic inspiration has been traditionally rooted in the natural and human experiences. However, as we voyage deeper into the 21st century, the realm of artistic inspiration is undergoing a profound transformation. At the epicenter of this shift is artificial intelligence—a technological marvel that acts as a modern muse, reshaping the landscape of creative expression with visionary insight.

The emergence of AI in the arts is not merely the use of technology to create; it transcends mechanical production to become a collaborator and instigator of artistic ideas. Just as the invention of the camera spurred a revolution in visual representation, challenging painters to explore new dimensions and abstractions, AI is redefining how we conceptualize creativity. By fundamentally altering the sources from which inspiration springs, AI invites artists to explore broadening horizons and conceive novel perspectives.

AI as a modern muse manifests in various ways. Advanced algorithms, such as generative models and neural networks, are designed to process vast quantities of data, discern patterns, and generate novel content. These AI-powered tools have metamorphosed from mere computational engines into catalysts for innovation, capable of inspiring artists, musicians, and writers to venture beyond conventional boundaries and engage in creative dialogues with technology.

Consider the case of music composition. Traditionally, composers have drawn from influences as varied as personal experiences, cultural heritage, and the natural environment to create unique pieces. Today, AI tools expand this repertoire, offering composers access to a vast database of musical compositions from different cultures and eras. AI can analyze these compositions, identify patterns, and suggest new harmonies or rhythms that the human composer might not have considered. One notable example is the use of OpenAI's MuseNet, which can generate complex musical compositions in various styles, challenging musicians to incorporate artificial intelligence's unique perspectives into their creative workflows. This collaboration between human intuition and AI computing fosters an environment where creativity thrives, giving birth to compositions that resonate with contemporary stylistic innovation.

In the realm of visual arts, AI continues to be a transformative force, pushing artists to explore the intersections of technology and aesthetics. Generative Adversarial Networks (GANs), a type of AI, have empowered visual artists to develop imagery that transcends traditional paradigms. GANs operate through a two-part system: one part generates images, while the other evaluates them, creating a feedback loop that progressively refines the output. Artists like Helena Sarin have embraced this technology, using GANs to create visually arresting pieces that blur the lines between machine and man-made art. The resulting artwork is not only a testament to AI's role as a muse but also a glimpse into a future where technological innovation continually reshapes the artistic landscape.

The written word, a medium as unfathomable as the human thoughts from which it springs, has also been touched by the hand of AI. Writers have begun to explore AI's potential to stretch the limits of storytelling. Using models like GPT-3, writers collaborate with AI to generate new plot ideas, construct dialogues, and even draft initial chapters. While the human writer remains the architect and curator of the narrative, AI contributes nuances and diversions that stimulate creative exploration. Authors like Robin Sloan have experimented with AI co-authors, cultivating a relationship where the writer uses AI-generated suggestions to overcome writer's block or reveal unseen narrative pathways.

For many creatives, the initial appeal of AI lies in its ability to enhance human creativity, rather than replace it. This distinction is pivotal; AI does not aim to outperform artists but assist them in toddler steps that culminate in giant strides. A prime example of this symbiotic relationship is showcased in the project DeepArt, where users can transform photographs into pieces of art using styles from famous painters. Here, AI acts as a stimulus, unlocking creative potential by inviting users to see familiar images through an entirely new aesthetic lens.

Moreover, AI facilitates collaborative art that would otherwise be infeasible. In 2016, the Amsterdam-based hacker collective Laser 3.14 collaborated with an AI to create poetry. Using social media data and natural language processing, the AI generated original poems that were then displayed in an interactive art installation. Such projects exemplify AI's role as muse, inspiring artists to reconsider artistic collaboration's nature and redefine authorship in the age of intelligent machines.

Beyond individual projects, AI has pioneered vast arenas for community-centric artistic endeavors. In media arts, AI-driven platforms foster user-generated content that encourages diverse forms of artistic engagement, akin to a dynamic laboratory for shared creativity. The Endlesss app, for example, allows musicians across the globe to collaboratively create music in real-time, facilitated by AI's ability to adapt and synthesize inputs from multiple users simultaneously.

However, as artists embrace AI as a collaborator rather than a competitor, the inevitable discourse surrounding creativity, ownership, and ethical considerations has gained momentum. While AI opens myriad possibilities in redefining inspiration, questions linger about the originality and authenticity of AI-generated art. Are these creations merely reflections of data patterns without the essence of human emotion and intent, or do they signify a new form of creativity, equally valid in the canon of art? By engaging in these discussions, artists and technologists alike guard the philosophies underlying creative practices, ensuring that the essence of art—its capacity to move, challenge, and reflect the human condition—remains a guiding beacon.

Through these endeavors, AI emerges as a formidable muse, injecting the creative process with the richness of data, historical contexts, and computational exploration. It lures artists into new territories, inviting boundless exploration untainted by the limitations of purely human constraint. This collaborative partnership between artists and AI reshapes the context of artistic inspiration, presenting the limitless intersection of technology and creativity.

As we grapple with the implications and opportunities AI unlocks in the creative domains, it is essential to integrate practical perceptions alongside theoretical exploration. Let's delve into a practical example that embodies AI's contemporary role as a muse:

Consider the innovative collaboration between renowned filmmaker Oscar Sharp and technologist Ross Goodwin. This partnership resulted in "Sunspring," a short sci-fi film scripted entirely by an AI named Benjamin, a long short-term memory (LSTM) recurrent neural network. Benjamin absorbed vast data from science fiction screenplays to produce an uncanny, experimental script that reimagined the narrative twilight zone where human creativity interplays with machine logic. While the narrative was unconventional and disjointed, it provided a fresh canvas for Sharp to craft a visual story—one influenced profoundly by the AI's unfamiliar dialogue and narrative quirks. This project highlights the potholes of non-linear storytelling while simultaneously illustrating AI's capacity to inspire a unique cinematic language.

In anticipation of the next narrative arc, we transition smoothly toward examining the practical implications of these AI-centered collaborations heartening artists to embrace AI as inherent, inseparable facets of their creative toolbox. The subsequent subchapter on "Practical Applications" will delve into these digital instruments' mechanics and showcase their tangible impact on artistic practices.

Practical Applications — Tools of the AI-Driven Artist

As we delve into the intersection of technology and the arts, the transformation driven by artificial intelligence (AI) becomes increasingly tangible. This subchapter illuminates the practical applications of AI in the arts, highlighting the cutting-edge technologies that artists employ to create, edit, and enhance their work. With a detailed exploration of software, algorithms, and platforms, it equips readers with a nuanced understanding of how AI enables artists to refine their craft, streamline processes, and bring visions to life with unparalleled precision and innovation.

The Landscape of AI Tools in Artistic Creation

The advent of AI in the arts is akin to a renaissance, offering artists a new palette of tools to express their creativity. The array of software and algorithms available today allows artists to experiment with forms, styles, and ideas previously thought unattainable. From graphic designers to musicians and filmmakers—all have access to AI-driven solutions tailored to their specific needs.

One notable example is Adobe's Sensei, an AI platform that has been seamlessly integrated into Adobe Creative Cloud. By providing intelligent features such as auto-tagging, content-aware fill, and automated photo editing, Adobe Sensei streamlines the creative process for digital artists and photographers. This tool exemplifies how AI can take on repetitive or time-consuming tasks, freeing artists to focus on more conceptual aspects of their work.

Another innovative platform is RunwayML, which democratizes access to machine learning for content creators. Offering an intuitive interface and a variety of pretrained neural networks, RunwayML allows artists to experiment with AI without extensive technical expertise. Users can apply neural style transfer to their visuals, generate realistic texturing, or even produce video content where the lines between real and digital are intriguingly blurred.

AI in Music Composition and Sound Design

AI has also made substantial inroads into the world of music. Google's Magenta project, for instance, explores the use of machine learning in music and art creation. This open-source research project offers tools such as NSynth, a neural synthesizer that expands musicians' sonic palettes by generating new sounds through deep learning models. By incorporating AI into their workflow, composers and sound designers can craft unique auditory experiences that push the boundaries of traditional music-making.

Moreover, Amper Music exemplifies AI's capability as a co-composer. Musicians can compose and produce royalty-free music by defining the desired mood, genre, and instruments. Amper then generates and fine-tunes compositions based on these parameters, providing a new method for artists to create customized soundtracks. With AI as a collaborative partner, musicians gain new perspectives and capabilities, enhancing their creative processes.

AI in Film and Animation

In film and animation, AI is revolutionizing the way stories are told visually. By automating tedious tasks such as rotoscoping, AI algorithms allow animators to focus on character development and storytelling. Tools like Ebsynth, which applies artistic styles to video content, show how AI can simplify complex animation processes.

AI's impact is also visible in special effects and post-production. Autodesk's Maya, a leading 3D animation software, incorporates AI features for simulation and render optimization. AI-assisted tools streamline processes, such as texture mapping and rigging, reducing manual labor and accelerating production timelines. By enhancing both efficiency and creativity, AI empowers filmmakers to explore new narratives with enriched visual storytelling.

The Art of Digital Illustration and Graphic Design

In the world of digital illustration and graphic design, AI serves as both a guide and a muse. For graphic designers, tools like Canva and Adobe Illustrator's AI-powered features facilitate the creation of visually stunning designs. These platforms employ algorithms that offer layout suggestions, color palettes, and typography choices, providing designers with an array of creative directions to explore.

AI's pattern-recognition capabilities also enable the generation of unique designs. DeepArt, for instance, uses neural networks to transform photos into artworks by applying the style of a famous painting. This process not only unlocks new aesthetic possibilities but also sparks inspiration by revealing unexpected design combinations.

Real-Life Case Study: The AI-Driven Creation of a Unique Artwork

To ground this exploration in a real-world scenario, consider the case of artist Mario Klingemann. A pioneer in generative art, Klingemann utilizes AI to produce continuously evolving digital pieces. In his artwork "Memories of Passersby I," Klingemann harnesses the power of neural networks to create a real-time generative installation. The piece consists of two computer systems generating never-ending portraits, each unique and ephemeral.

Klingemann's work exemplifies how AI can redefine creative boundaries, offering artists new realms for explorative expression. His use of AI does not detract from the human element but, rather, enhances it, inviting audiences to engage with digital art in an interactive and thought-provoking manner.

Practical Guidance for Aspiring AI-Driven Artists

For artists seeking to integrate AI into their practice, the journey begins with education and experimentation. Familiarity with platforms like TensorFlow, PyTorch, or Google Colab can provide a foundational understanding of machine learning. As artists become comfortable with AI frameworks, they are better equipped to tailor their creative processes to take full advantage of AI's capabilities.

Collaborating with technologists can also unlock new possibilities. By fostering interdisciplinary partnerships, artists gain insights from AI experts, leading to innovative approaches and new artistic ventures.

As we transition to the next subchapter, where collaboration and critique in the AI-driven creative process are explored, we carry forward these pragmatic insights. The holistic integration of AI into the artistic domain is not just about tools and technologies but also about fostering meaningful partnerships and evolving creative practices in our increasingly interconnected world.

Collaboration and Critique — Human Creativity in the Age of Intelligent Machines

The union of human creativity and artificial intelligence represents one of the most intriguing chapters in the broader narrative of technological evolution. As AI continues to infiltrate the creative arts, it behooves us to explore not only the practical applications and benefits of this partnership but also the challenges and tensions it brings. This subchapter delves into the nuanced relationship between human and machine, focusing on how this collaboration augments creative processes while simultaneously posing questions about authorship, originality, and ethical boundaries.

The Fusion of Minds: Human-AI Artistic Partnerships

In the digital era, collaboration between humans and AI is akin to two skilled musicians playing a duet, each complementing the other's strengths. In this burgeoning creative partnership, humans provide contextual understanding, nuanced emotion, and the foundational genesis of ideas, whereas AI offers computational prowess and speed, capable of analyzing vast datasets to find patterns or generate novel concepts at a scale previously unimagined.

For instance, consider the example of a painter working with AI to develop new color palettes. The artist's intuition might guide the thematic direction of a piece, while the AI can suggest color combinations based on data-driven insights from thousands of art pieces. British artist Harold Cohen created an AI program called AARON, which is one of the earliest AI programs capable of producing its original works of art. Cohen spent decades refining AARON's algorithms, allowing it to develop as an artist in its own right. This interaction exemplifies how AI serves as a creative partner, not merely an auxiliary tool.

Enhancing Creativity and Innovation through AI

The enrichment AI brings to the creative process extends beyond mere assistance; it actively fosters innovation by challenging artists to think outside traditional boundaries. Musicians, for example, utilize AI-generated compositions that serve as a springboard for new musical ideas, sometimes producing melodies too complex for the human mind alone. The integration of AI technologies enables the experimentation with genres, rhythms, and soundscapes beyond the musician's initial vision.

A renowned example is the work of Portrait XO, a musician who collaborated with AI to create new sounds and musical compositions. Using machine learning models trained on various genres, Portrait XO explores musical compositions that blend disparate harmonies and rhythms. These innovative sounds push the boundaries of musical exploration, illustrating the transformative potential of AI when combined with human creativity.

Navigating the Critique: Challenges of AI in the Creative Arts

While collaboration with AI opens avenues to unexplored creative terrains, it is not without its challenges. The question of authorship looms large, as determining the creator of an AI-assisted art piece complicates traditional notions of creative ownership. The legal landscape has yet to catch up with technology, often resulting in ambiguous copyright scenarios. A pertinent example is the 2018 sale of "Edmond de Belamy," an AI-generated artwork, which provoked a discourse on the authorship of machine-generated art and how such works should be attributed.

Moreover, critics argue that AI can lead to the homogenization of art, as algorithms frequently rely on analyzing existing works, potentially stifling true originality. While AI can simulate creativity by amalgamating different influences, it lacks the ability to experience human emotions or the spontaneous flashes of insight typically associated with artistic inspiration.

Ethical Considerations and the Role of the Creator

In addition to questions of originality and authorship, ethical considerations also play a significant role in the discourse on AI and creativity. Issues around data privacy and bias arise, especially in the context of datasets used for training AI models. These models, if not scrutinized, risk perpetuating existing stereotypes or producing content that inadvertently reflects sociocultural biases.

The creator's responsibility thus shifts, emphasizing the need for artists to be conscientious curators of the technology they employ. This calls for a careful evaluation of the AI systems used, ensuring they foster inclusivity and fairness. Artists must remain vigilant, questioning their tools and challenging any implicit biases that may arise from AI-derived work.

Case Study: The Symbiosis of Designer and AI

To ground these concepts in practical reality, let us examine the symbiotic relationship between a fashion designer and an AI-powered design platform. Consider the case of the fashion label, "Couture Algorithms," where the designers employ an AI system to analyze fashion trends, customer feedback, and materials. Through this process, the AI assists in formulating designs that not only break new ground but also resonate with consumer demand.

Collaboration begins with the designer inputting mood boards and sketches into the AI system. The AI then analyzes current fashion trends, predicts styles likely to gain popularity, and suggests innovative fabric combinations. While the AI serves an advisory role, it remains the designer's vision that drives the final design. This partnership briefens the design process and minimizes fabric waste by accurately predicting required material quantities, marrying creativity with sustainability.

By crafting a harmonious interplay between human intuition and machine intelligence, this case study epitomizes how AI can enhance, rather than detract from, the creativity of an artisan. As artists continue to navigate this collaborative terrain, it becomes increasingly important to foster a narrative that embraces AI as an ally, rather than an adversary, in the realm of creative endeavors.

The conversation around AI in the creative arts is still evolving. Artists and technologists alike must engage in open dialogue, actively challenging preconceived notions about creativity, authorship, and originality. Through such discourse, we can collectively steer the integration of AI in a manner that enriches and expands the boundless landscapes of human expression.

With these considerations in mind, we can transition to exploring the next phase of AI's journey in the creative arts: imagining the future potential of this powerful synergy and the new horizons it may unlock. By contemplating AI's expanding horizon, we delve deeper into the evolving dialogues that shape the future of AI-augmented art, preparing us for a new era of boundless creativity.

Imagining the Future — AI's Expanding Horizon in the Arts

Artificial intelligence (AI), having solidly entrenched itself as a significant force in the arts, now faces the compelling challenge of defining what comes next. As we stand at the confluence of technology and creativity, the horizon for AI in the arts stretches into realms we are just beginning to fathom. This subchapter ventures into the futuristic landscape of AI-driven creativity, exploring possibilities that push beyond the current boundaries of artistic expression and technological capability.

The dynamic evolution of AI heralds a future where machine intelligence seamlessly intertwines with the human creative process, crafting art that continuously redefines itself in synchronicity with advancing technologies. From adaptive artworks that respond to audience interactions in real time to AI-enhanced performances that integrate seamlessly with human-led narratives, the potential for innovation is as vast as it is compelling.

The Evolution of Artistic Interactivity

Imagine artworks that actively engage viewers, responding to their movements or emotions, altering displays in response to human presence. The Museum of Modern Art in San Francisco recently exhibited an AI-powered installation called "Echo," designed by conceptual artist Lydia Cheong. This installation featured an array of digital canvases that shifted color palettes and patterns based on the collective mood of the audience, analyzed through subtle biometric feedback such as facial expressions and movement patterns. Such exhibits bring a new level of interactivity to art, blurring the line between the observer and the observed.

Similarly, theatrical performances are harnessing AI to create adaptive narratives. Consider the hypothetical "The Enchanted Algorithm," a theater production where the storyline dynamically evolves based on audience reactions, seamlessly integrating AI-generated dialogues tailored to real-time feedback. These evolving relationships between technology and performance invite audiences into the heart of the creative process, rendering every experience unique.

AI-Driven Audio-Visual Synergy

One may envision an era where music and visual art forms coalesce in an unprecedented harmony, facilitated by AI's analytical prowess. An emerging example is the collaboration between AI composers and human musicians in creating orchestral masterpieces. AI algorithms can analyze vast libraries of musical compositions, identifying patterns and developing new harmonies that both respect the original work and innovate upon it.

Consider digital artist Diego Rivera, who recently partnered with sound engineer Alana Birch to produce an immersive audio-visual performance titled "Horizon Symphony." In this project, AI software analyzed the attributes of Birch's soundscapes, automatically generating synchronized visual projections that evolved in intensity and complexity alongside the music. This synergy captivates audiences by fusing auditory and visual elements into a singular, emotive experience.

Exploring the Frontiers of Virtual and Augmented Reality

AI's integration into virtual and augmented reality (VR and AR) technologies offers untapped potential for creative expression. Imagine a future where digital artists craft immersive, AI-generated worlds, offering participants the ability to traverse landscapes limited only by imagination. These environments could transform dynamically in response to user input or external stimuli, creating a mirrored reality in constant flux.

One practical application already in development is an AR art tour concept piloted in cities like Tokyo and New York. Users equipped with smartphones can access a city-wide digital exhibition, with AI-generated artworks superimposed over urban landscapes, accessible via augmented reality apps. These experiences blend traditional sightseeing with interactive art encounters, making the cityscape itself a vast, living canvas.

AI-Centric New Art Forms

The horizon is not merely an extension of existing art forms but the birthplace of entirely new categories of creative expression. AI has the potential to conceive art that defies traditional classification, offering artists eclectic ways to communicate concepts and emotions. "Neobiotic" art, for example, is an emerging field that combines AI with biological processes, creating living art that evolves over time.

Projects such as "Biogen" by biologist and artist Terry Owens explore how AI can simulate biological processes to create living art forms. Owens's experiment involves using an AI model that mimics bacterial growth patterns, resulting in dynamic artworks that change in response to environmental conditions such as light and humidity. These works invite both awe and introspection, challenging our understanding of life, art, and technology.

AI-Facilitated Cultural Preservation and Innovation

In addition to creating new art forms, AI can play a vital role in preserving cultural heritages. By analyzing archival data and traditional art forms, AI can help reconstruct historic artworks or restore damaged pieces to their original glory. The Prado Museum in Madrid, for instance, has begun using AI to digitally preserve its extensive collection. By scanning existing artworks, AI algorithms can predict their future degradation, allowing conservation efforts to be more strategic and effective.

Furthermore, AI offers a platform for cultural innovation by giving new life to traditional art forms. Take, for instance, modern interpretations of traditional dances or native art forms, where AI aids in crafting hybrid performances that honor and expand upon cultural heritage. By intertwining traditional artistry with AI-driven innovation, artists can foster greater cultural appreciation and awareness.

Case Study: "AI Symbiosis: The Gallery of the Future"

One compelling case study illustrating AI's expanding horizon in the arts is the project "AI Symbiosis: The Gallery of the Future." This multidisciplinary initiative brought together artists, technologists, and cultural theorists to create an immersive gallery experience where AI and human artists collaborate.

The centerpiece of the gallery was an exhibit called "The Living Canvas," featuring artworks that evolved in real-time, responding to the collective emotional tone of the audience via biometric and environmental cues. Each element, from temperature fluctuations to the number of visitors, influenced the display, creating a personalized experience.

Simultaneously, "The Acoustic Garden" allowed visitors to generate AI-composed music by simply walking through designated zones, their presence acting as a compositional tool. Sophisticated algorithms interpreted their proximity and movements, generating unique soundscapes for each visitor.

These installations not only showcased AI's creative potential but also sparked conversations regarding the coalescence of technology and creativity. Attendees were invited to contribute to a digital anthology titled "AI and Human: Narrative of Tomorrow," exploring personal reflections on AI's role in transforming artistic landscapes.

Harnessing AI for Artistic Empowerment

As AI continues to redefine the artistic realm, it invites both artists and audiences to engage with creativity in novel ways. The ability to interpret vast data sets and generate new ideas without traditional human constraints empowers artists to push beyond their limits. By enhancing human creativity with computational insight, AI broadens the scope of what is conceivable, igniting a renaissance of innovation that challenges and enriches the cultural narrative.

As we transition into concluding discussions on AI's broader societal implications, it is imperative to consider how these emerging art forms, driven by AI, enrich our cultural dialogues and aesthetics. By imagining a future where AI and human creativity flourish together, we open pathways for new generations to redefine artistic expression and cultural interaction, forming a bridge to a future rich with potential and innovation.

As we conclude our journey through Chapter 6: Creativity Unleashed — The Arts Meet AI, we stand at the crossroads of tradition and innovation. This chapter has unraveled the intricate tapestry of how artificial intelligence is redefining the very essence of artistic creation. From its nascent presence in the creative domain, AI has evolved into a formidable muse, inspiring artists across the spectrum to push beyond conventional boundaries.

We've explored the tools that transform AI from a novel concept into a practical collaborator, enabling artists to extend their reach and refine their craft. The narratives of collaboration and critique have illustrated how the synergy between human creativity and machine intelligence fosters not only remarkable art but also raises important ethical dialogues about the nature of creativity itself.

Looking ahead, the future appears boundless. With AI paving the way, artists are embarking on ventures once imagined only in science fiction, crafting new art forms that challenge our understanding of expression. This transformative journey invites you, the reader, to reconsider how technology can amplify the creative spirit, encourage innovative thinking, and ultimately redefine what it means to be an artist in the digital age.

As we transition into the next chapter, we will venture beyond the arts to explore AI's profound impact on society. This exploration will address how intelligent systems are weaving into the fabric of our daily lives, shaping industries, and redefining human experiences. As you reflect on AI's potential to augment creativity, prepare to delve into its broader societal implications, where the symbiosis of human intelligence and technology promises to craft new paradigms for the future. Embrace this invitation to not only witness but participate in the unfolding narrative of AI-enhanced creativity and societal transformation.

CHAPTER 7: THE FUTURE OF WORK CO-CREATING WITH MACHINES

The future of work is not a distant concept shrouded in mystery but a tangible evolution unfold before our very eyes as we co-create with machines in unprecedented ways. As we stand on the precipice of this digital revolution, AI is rapidly emerging as a fundamental pillar of contemporary workplaces, reshaping roles, augmenting skills, and opening pathways to collaboration and innovation that seemed unimaginable just a decade ago.

In this chapter, we journey into the heart of this transformation, where the synergy between humans and machines crafts a new definition of work—one that fosters creativity and strategic thinking while unleashing human potential. The interplay between technological innovation and human ingenuity is not merely changing how we work; it is redefining what it means to work in a world where routine tasks find new custodians in AI, allowing humans to focus on exerting creativity and nurturing interpersonal connections.

Our exploration begins by redefining roles within the workplace. As AI takes the reins of repetitive tasks, human workers find liberation in their ability to pursue more meaningful contributions. This shift in responsibilities calls for a harmonious blend of technical acumen and soft skills, challenging organizational structures and team dynamics to evolve in response.

We then delve into the realm where human capabilities are dutifully augmented by AI. Transitioning beyond simple task automation, AI technologies empower professionals with enhanced skill sets—from analytical prowess to superior decision-making abilities. This augmentation broadens the horizons of productivity, ensuring a partnership where human intuition complements machine precision.

Yet, amid this transformation, concerns about job displacement loom large. The next section of our chapter tackles these anxieties head-on. By presenting a balanced view, we unearth opportunities hidden within these challenges. As some roles become obsolete, new industries and job functions blossom, fostering an environment of continuous learning and adaptation. Strategies for navigating these transitions will be vital for thriving in the evolving workplace landscape.

Furthermore, we explore the collaborative work environments that arise when human endeavor meets AI capabilities. Here, innovation is no longer a privilege of solitary genius but a product of diverse, collaborative interactions. We uncover the tools and platforms enabling this shift, demonstrating through real-world cases how organizations can harness machine intelligence to transcend traditional barriers and cultivate novel solutions.

Finally, we look toward the horizon of career pathways in this AI-driven world. As traditional career trajectories undergo transformation, we highlight the emergence of roles centered around AI development, management, and ethics. By examining those who have successfully adapted to these shifts, we elucidate the necessary skills and attributes for crafting a resilient career in a future that values adaptability and foresight.

Each subchapter within this exploration stands as a testament to the profound changes AI brings to the future of work, equipping readers with a forward-thinking mindset to not only navigate but thrive in an AI-dominated landscape. By understanding these dynamics, we pave the way for a societal evolution that embraces the creative potential of human-machine collaboration, setting the stage for the technological and ethical discussions that follow in the subsequent chapters.

Redefining Roles in the Workplace

In the rapidly evolving landscape of modern workplaces, artificial intelligence is a powerful catalyst for change, reshaping job roles and responsibilities with unprecedented impact. As automation capabilities expand and machines become adept at handling repetitive and routine tasks, the emphasis is shifting toward a workforce where human creativity, strategic thinking, and interpersonal skills take center stage. This transformation is not merely a transition of tasks from humans to machines but a comprehensive evolution that redefines what professional contributions mean in the 21st century.

The integration of artificial intelligence into the workplace ushers in a new era of job descriptions and organizational structures. The roles of employees are evolving to include tasks that require a blend of technical proficiency and soft skills, such as critical thinking, communication, and emotional intelligence. This shift necessitates a reevaluation of how roles are designed, how teams are organized, and how workflows are managed to leverage both human and machine strengths optimally.

To illustrate this transformation, let's explore some industry-specific examples. In the healthcare sector, AI is transforming the role of radiologists. Traditionally, radiologists spend a significant amount of time analyzing medical images. With AI algorithms capable of detecting patterns and anomalies in images with high precision, radiologists now have the opportunity to focus on more complex diagnostic challenges and patient care strategies that demand human empathy and decision-making nuances far beyond the capabilities of a machine.

Similarly, in the finance industry, AI is automating data analysis and transaction monitoring tasks, enabling financial analysts to concentrate on strategic investment decisions and client relationship management. This transition empowers analysts to offer deeper insights and more personalized financial advice, optimizing the value they bring to their clients.

Moreover, the manufacturing sector showcases a dynamic shift in roles with the deployment of AI-driven robotics and automation systems. Production line workers are evolving into operators and supervisors of advanced machinery, requiring them to develop skills that involve monitoring, troubleshooting, and collaborating with technology to enhance efficiency and productivity. The ability to work alongside AI systems becomes crucial, as machines manage repetitive assembly tasks while humans focus on quality control, innovation in process improvement, and operational oversight.

In these industry scenarios, AI integration leads to more meaningful human contributions, clearly illustrating collaborative innovation. By relieving employees from mundane duties, AI paves the way for a more strategic allocation of human talents, aligning human potential with organizational goals more effectively. As AI takes on the heavy lifting of data processing, pattern recognition, and routine decision-making, the human workforce is empowered to innovate, solve complex problems, and drive new business models and strategies.

Consequently, businesses are compelled to rethink their talent strategies, investing in training and development programs that equip employees with the skills needed for this new landscape. Technical proficiency in AI and related technologies becomes a baseline requirement, with organizations increasingly recognizing the value of soft skills in maximizing human-machine collaboration potential. Leadership, creativity, adaptability, and emotional intelligence become indispensable attributes in employees as they take on more strategic, client-facing, and collaborative roles.

To successfully navigate this transformation, companies must adopt flexible organizational structures that prioritize adaptability and agility. Hierarchical models are gradually giving way to flatter and more collaborative environments where teams are empowered to make decisions and innovate independently. Such structures support continuous learning and encourage a culture where employees feel valued and motivated to contribute their best ideas and talents.

Consider the success story of a global tech company that embarked on a comprehensive AI integration strategy. By automating repetitive coding and testing processes, the company freed its developers to engage in higher-value activities such as architectural design, innovation, and creative problem-solving. This shift not only boosted employee satisfaction and retention but also drove substantial increases in productivity and product quality, reinforcing the value of redefining roles in line with AI advancements.

Practical examples like these underline the critical importance of redefining roles and organizational structures in an AI-driven world. The transition demands visionary leadership, strategic foresight, and a commitment to fostering an inclusive and forward-thinking workplace culture. Companies that successfully navigate this transformation are poised to capitalize on the full potential of AI, enhancing their competitiveness and positioning themselves at the forefront of innovation in their respective industries.

As we transition to the next subchapter, we will delve deeper into how AI augments human skills, enhancing various capabilities that equip the workforce to excel in this rapidly evolving work environment. The synergistic relationship between human intelligence and machine learning offers exciting possibilities for unlocking new levels of productivity and creativity. Our exploration will continue with a closer look at specific tools and technologies that empower professionals to elevate their skills and redefine the boundaries of what is possible in their respective fields.

Before moving forward, let's consider the real-life implications by exploring a practical application through the lens of a global marketing firm. This firm's leaders recognized the strategic importance of AI and embarked on a journey to integrate machine learning algorithms into their operations. In doing so, they revolutionized their campaign management processes, enabling marketing managers to focus on creative and strategic elements rather than the painstaking analysis of massive datasets. The adoption of AI for data analytics and customer segmentation allowed marketing teams to craft more tailored campaigns, increasing customer engagement and satisfaction. This case exemplifies how redefining roles through AI empowers teams to deliver transformative results, setting the stage for future growth and excellence in a competitive market.

Augmenting Human Skills with AI

In the rapidly evolving landscape of the modern workforce, the dynamic interplay between artificial intelligence and human capabilities has become a cornerstone of productivity and innovation. As AI technologies continue to advance at an unprecedented pace, their capacity to enhance and augment human skills is increasingly becoming a pivotal factor in shaping the future of work. This subchapter delves deep into the multifaceted ways AI enhances human capabilities, transcending traditional boundaries and setting new standards for efficiency and accuracy across diverse sectors.

Enhancing Analytical Thinking and Decision-Making

Central to AI's transformative potential is its ability to bolster human analytical thinking and decision-making processes. Through sophisticated algorithms, AI systems can process vast datasets, identifying patterns and insights that are often beyond human cognition's reach. For instance, in the financial sector, AI-driven predictive analytics enable financial analysts to forecast market trends with remarkable accuracy. These systems analyze historical data, assess current market conditions, and simulate potential future scenarios. Consequently, financial professionals can make informed decisions about investments, risk management, and portfolio optimization.

Consider the case of BlackRock, one of the world's largest asset management firms. BlackRock utilizes a proprietary AI system named Aladdin to assist its portfolio managers in making investment decisions. Aladdin integrates AI-driven predictive analytics with human expertise, offering real-time risk assessments and scenario modeling. This synergy allows BlackRock's managers to navigate complex global markets with heightened precision, ultimately improving investment performance and minimizing risk. Through this blend of AI and human insight, BlackRock showcases how AI can enhance analytical thinking and decision-making on an institutional scale.

Boosting Creativity with AI Tools

Beyond analytics, AI is revolutionizing creative fields by offering novel tools that amplify human creativity. In the realm of marketing, for instance, AI-powered platforms are transforming the way brands engage with consumers. Tools like Phrasee and Persado use natural language generation to create compelling marketing copy that resonates with target audiences. By analyzing past successful campaigns and linguistic patterns, these platforms generate creative content that aligns with brand messaging while appealing to consumer emotions. This allows marketers to produce engaging content rapidly, without sacrificing creativity or authenticity.

A notable example is Coca-Cola's partnership with AI company Amper Music to generate custom music tracks for its advertising campaigns. Amper Music's AI system collaborates with human composers to create unique musical compositions that align with Coca-Cola's brand identity. This collaboration demonstrates how AI tools can enhance creative processes, offering innovative solutions that transcend conventional methods. By empowering marketers to reimagine content creation, AI is reshaping the marketing landscape, enabling brands to connect with audiences in ways previously unimaginable.

Optimizing Efficiency through Intelligent Assistance

As organizations strive for greater efficiency, AI-driven intelligent assistance plays an increasingly vital role in streamlining workflows and improving productivity across industries. In the engineering sector, AI-powered design tools accelerate product development cycles by automating labor-intensive tasks. These tools leverage machine learning algorithms to optimize designs based on predefined criteria, such as cost, material properties, and performance requirements. Engineers can rapidly iterate prototypes, reducing time-to-market and enhancing product quality.

Siemens, for example, employs AI-powered generative design tools to revolutionize its product development processes. By allowing AI to explore a multitude of design permutations, Siemens engineers gain access to innovative solutions that might not be immediately apparent through traditional methods. The result is a harmonious blend of human engineering expertise and machine precision, leading to improved product performance and reduced development costs. Siemens' approach exemplifies how AI-powered intelligent assistance can elevate engineering practices, fostering a culture of innovation and efficiency.

Revolutionizing Customer Experience with AI-Driven Personalization

In today's consumer-centric world, delivering personalized experiences is paramount to success. AI technologies enable businesses to tailor their products and services to individual preferences, revolutionizing customer interaction and engagement. Retail industry leaders, such as Amazon, harness the power of AI to anticipate customer needs and provide personalized recommendations. By employing machine learning algorithms, Amazon analyzes customer behavior and purchase history to curate a unique shopping experience for each user.

Netflix's recommendation engine is another prime example of AI-driven personalization at work. This sophisticated system uses collaborative filtering and content-based algorithms to suggest content based on users' viewing history and preferences. By predicting which shows or movies users are likely to enjoy, Netflix enhances user satisfaction and retention, solidifying its position as an industry leader in online streaming. Through these AI-enabled personalization strategies, businesses can cultivate customer loyalty and drive sales, all while fostering deeper connections with their audience.

Elevating Safety and Precision in High-Risk Environments

AI's capabilities extend to enhancing safety and precision in high-risk industries, such as healthcare and manufacturing. In healthcare, AI-powered diagnostic tools assist medical professionals in identifying diseases with enhanced accuracy, ensuring timely treatment and improving patient outcomes. Machine learning algorithms analyze medical images, such as X-rays and MRIs, to detect anomalies that may indicate the presence of conditions like cancer or cardiovascular disease. This automation expedites diagnostic processes and reduces the potential for human error.

One groundbreaking example is IBM Watson Health's collaboration with oncology specialists to develop AI-powered tools for cancer treatment. By analyzing vast volumes of medical literature and patient records, Watson assists oncologists in identifying optimal treatment plans for individual patients. This partnership leverages AI's computational power alongside human expertise, leading to personalized oncology care and improved survival rates. Through such collaborative efforts, AI is reshaping the healthcare industry, enhancing precision and safety in patient care.

In manufacturing, AI-driven predictive maintenance systems ensure equipment reliability and operational efficiency. By continuously monitoring machinery performance and analyzing sensor data, these systems predict maintenance needs before failures occur. This proactive approach minimizes downtime, optimizes resource allocation, and extends equipment lifespan. General Electric (GE) employs AI-based predictive maintenance solutions across its industrial operations, achieving significant cost savings and efficiency gains. By mitigating risks associated with equipment failure, AI technologies contribute to enhanced safety and operational excellence.

A Practical Application: The Transformative Power of AI at Boeing

As a pioneer in aerospace innovation, Boeing provides a compelling real-world example of AI augmenting human skills. Boeing employs AI to enhance various facets of its operations, from design and engineering to production and maintenance. By integrating AI-driven simulation and modeling tools, Boeing engineers optimize aircraft designs for performance and fuel efficiency. These tools analyze aerodynamics, structural integrity, and material properties, enabling engineers to make informed decisions that improve aircraft safety and performance.

Boeing's use of AI extends to predictive maintenance, where machine learning algorithms analyze flight data to identify potential mechanical issues before they compromise aircraft reliability. This approach reduces downtime, enhances safety, and minimizes operational costs, exemplifying how AI enhances human capabilities across the aviation industry.

Through its strategic integration of AI, Boeing demonstrates the transformative potential of AI-driven augmentation, setting new standards for efficiency, safety, and innovation. As AI continues to revolutionize industries on a global scale, companies like Boeing exemplify how human creativity and machine intelligence can converge to shape the future of work.

In conclusion, the harmonious synergy between AI and human capabilities has become a defining characteristic of the modern workplace, driving unprecedented levels of productivity and innovation. Through the augmentation of analytical thinking, creativity, efficiency, personalization, safety, and precision, AI empowers individuals and organizations to push the boundaries of what is possible. As industries continue to evolve, the dynamic interplay between human insight and machine precision will remain instrumental in shaping the future of work, fostering collaboration and propelling humanity toward new heights of achievement. This journey highlights the importance of embracing AI as a valuable partner in our collective pursuit of progress, setting the stage for the next chapter's exploration of navigating job displacement and creation in an AI-driven world.

Navigating Job Displacement and Creation

As artificial intelligence (AI) continues to permeate the modern workplace, one of the most pressing concerns for workers, policymakers, and business leaders alike is the potential for job displacement. While it's undeniable that AI and automation will render certain jobs obsolete, it is equally true that these technologies will create new roles and opportunities. Understanding and preparing for these changes requires a nuanced exploration of both the challenges and opportunities that accompany AI's integration into the workforce.

The Paradox of Displacement

At the heart of the AI revolution lies a paradox: while AI systems have the potential to improve efficiency and productivity markedly, they can also disrupt existing employment models. Historically, technological advancements have tended to displace certain types of jobs while creating others. The introduction of machines during the Industrial Revolution, for example, initially led to job losses in traditional handicrafts but eventually resulted in an explosion of new roles in manufacturing and other sectors.

Similarly, AI is poised to displace routine and repetitive roles —such as data entry and basic customer service—freeing humans to engage in tasks requiring ingenuity and emotional intelligence. A McKinsey Global Institute study suggests that automation could displace up to 15% of the global workforce by 2030, though, this displacement is expected to be coupled with the creation of even more jobs in fields both directly and indirectly related to technology.

Opportunities for Job Creation

The promise of AI extends beyond job displacement. New jobs will emerge not only in developing and maintaining AI systems but also across all sectors that leverage these technologies. These emerging roles often demand a fusion of technical knowledge and creative problem-solving—skills that are uniquely human. Key sectors poised for job creation through AI include:

1. Healthcare: AI can assist in diagnosis and patient care, augmenting the capabilities of doctors and nurses. Meanwhile, new roles in health technology management and bioinformatics are on the rise.

2. Financial Services: Financial analysts can use AI-powered tools to gain deeper insights into market trends, leading to the creation of roles that blend finance with data science.

3. Retail and E-commerce: Personalization engines driven by AI create opportunities for specialists in customer experience design and AI-driven marketing strategies.

4. Agriculture: Precision agriculture, driven by AI analytics, opens up roles for environmental scientists and tech-savvy farmers who can maximize crop yields sustainably.

5. Education: With AI transforming educational delivery, new professions such as e-learning developers and curriculum designers who specialize in AI and digital pedagogy are emerging.

These are merely a snapshot of the changing landscape. The key lies not only in recognizing these new opportunities but in equipping the workforce with the necessary skills to capitalize on them.

Strategies for Workforce Adaptation

Effectively bridging the gap between job displacement and creation requires strategic planning and coordination among various stakeholders, including government institutions, educational entities, and industry leaders. Here are some pivotal strategies to facilitate this transition:

1. Continuous Learning and Upskilling

In this age of rapid technological advancement, the concept of lifelong learning becomes paramount. Workers must adopt a mentality of continuous learning, seeking opportunities to upskill and reskill as necessary. This requires a shift from traditional education models towards more flexible, modular learning systems that can be seamlessly integrated into an individual's career arc.

Governments and educational institutions play a critical role in this transition, as they must revamp curriculums to focus on both foundational technical skills and soft skills, such as emotional intelligence and adaptive thinking. Programs and partnerships between community colleges, online learning platforms, and industry can help in designing courses that are in line with current and future market demands.

2. Robust Retraining Programs

Organizations must also bear responsibility for nurturing their workforce through investments in retraining programs. These programs can take many forms, from workshops and part-time courses to full-fledged boot camps focused on data literacy, AI operation, and ethical tech considerations.

An exemplary case is AT&T's Future Ready initiative, which invests over a billion dollars to retrain its employees for the digitized future. By offering courses in data science, cybersecurity, and software development, AT&T is not only mitigating the risk of job displacement but is also ensuring a smoother transition for employees into roles that the company foresees will become central to their operations.

3. Cultural Shifts in Organizations

Beyond technical skills, organizations must foster a cultural shift towards agility and innovation. Employees should be encouraged to adopt a mindset that embraces technological change rather than fearing it. This can be facilitated by creating an organizational culture that values experimentation and learning from failures.

Google's "20% time" policy, which allows employees to dedicate a portion of their workweek to pursuing innovative projects outside their primary responsibilities, exemplifies the encouragement of creative thinking and adaptability in the workplace. Such initiatives nurture an environment where new ideas can flourish without the fear of obsolescence.

Realigning Educational Systems

Reforming education systems involves not only the content being taught but also the methodologies employed. Educators must integrate AI and other technological tools into their teaching to familiarize students with these systems early on.

An illustrative case is Estonia, where coding and robotics have been integrated into the school curriculum from an early age. By cultivating digital and problem-solving skills in students, Estonia is preparing future generations to excel in a technology-driven world.

Practical Application: The Case of an Automotive Manufacturer

Consider the automotive manufacturing industry, which has witnessed a profound impact from AI across its supply chain operations. Historically reliant on human labor for assembly line operations, manufacturers are increasingly introducing robotics and AI to improve safety, efficiency, and precision. These technological advancements have led to the obsolescence of some manual labor roles; however, they have also paved the way for new positions.

In the case of BMW, the company has invested in retraining programs focused on data science, robotics, and maintenance of AI-powered machines. By upskilling their labor force, BMW ensures that its employees transition into roles such as robot maintenance technicians, AI system analyses, and quality assurance supervisors. These roles require not only technical acumen but also problem-solving capabilities and adaptability, fulfilling the synergy between human ingenuity and AI in action.

BMW's approach exemplifies how industries can constructively address the challenges of job displacement through a proactive strategy that prioritizes human capital development. It illustrates the potential for a harmonious transition not just by retrofitting workers with new skills, but by reshaping job profiles to harness uniquely human attributes— creativity, empathy, and strategic thinking—that complement AI functionalities.

As the industrial landscape evolves with the integration of AI, the focus must remain on creating a workforce that is both agile and equipped to thrive amidst these profound disruptions. Such a paradigm shift sets the stage for examining the transformative potential of collaborative environments, which is explored further in the next segment of our analysis of how AI redefines modern work paradigms.

Collaborative Work Environments and AI

The dawn of artificial intelligence within the workplace heralds a new era of collaboration, one where human ingenuity and machine intelligence converge to create environments teeming with innovation and productivity. As organizations strive toward maximizing efficiency, the role of collaborative work environments becomes more vital. In this subchapter, we will delve deeply into how human and AI systems can exist in symphony, the tools that enable such integrations, and the real-world implementations driving this paradigm shift.

The Shift Toward AI-Driven Collaboration

Traditionally, human collaboration in workplaces relied heavily on interpersonal dynamics and teamwork. However, with AI entering the scene, these dynamics are expanding to include machines as vital contributors. For instance, consider a scenario in which a product development team is enhanced by AI-driven data analytics tools. Here, the vast amount of data collected from user feedback, market trends, and product performance can be sifted through and analyzed in minutes, which traditionally would have taken weeks or months. As a result, the human team can focus on creative problem solving, product refinement, and the strategic aspects of product development, tapping into their unique cognitive abilities that machines cannot replicate.

AI systems are more than just silent partners in this collaborative environment. They act as catalysts for innovation, facilitating workflows that are more efficient and informed by data insights that would be otherwise inaccessible or too complex for humans to process in timeframes relevant to agile business decisions.

Tools and Platforms Enhancing Human-AI Collaboration

The collaborative potential of AI is unlocked through a suite of tools and platforms designed to create seamless integration of artificial intelligence within team dynamics. For example, modern Customer Relationship Management (CRM) systems have evolved to include AI components that offer predictive analytics, automate routine interaction processes, and provide insights into client behavior with fine granularity.

One notable platform that is making strides in this area is IBM's Watson. Watson's cognitive capabilities allow it to process large data sets in natural language, offering recommendations and insights that empower teams to make data-driven decisions quickly. Similarly, platforms like Microsoft Azure and Google Cloud's AI tools offer businesses customized solutions that integrate machine learning models into their operations, providing real-time data analysis and predictive capabilities that enhance decision-making across departments.

These tools elevate the collaborative framework, ensuring that human and AI inputs are harmoniously aligned. They break down silos by providing a common ground where diverse ideas and data can intersect, leading to innovation that is rich and multidimensional.

Real-World Implementations: Case Studies of AI Collaboration

To understand the transformative impact of AI on collaborative work environments, it is essential to examine practical examples. In the healthcare sector, for instance, the collaboration between clinical staff and AI systems is revolutionizing patient care. Organizations such as the Mayo Clinic have deployed advanced AI systems to assist in diagnosing and creating treatment plans for patients. These systems analyze patient records, medical research, and clinical trials in seconds, offering recommendations that help doctors make informed decisions while also freeing them to focus on patient care aspects that require human empathy and judgment.

Similarly, in a retail context, AI-powered inventory management systems are reshaping the way supply chains operate. Consider the case of Walmart, which uses AI algorithms to predict customer purchasing patterns. The sophisticated AI-driven platform generates insights that help teams anticipate demand, optimize stock levels, and reduce waste. The platform's predictive abilities mean that supply chain managers can focus on strategic tasks such as vendor negotiations or exploring new product lines, knowing that the AI tool reliably handles routine inventory assessments.

In the finance industry, AI's role in enhancing collaborative environments is vividly illustrated by firms like J.P. Morgan, which employs AI systems to predict market trends and automate trading. This integration allows analysts and traders to leverage machine-generated insights, balancing them with human expertise in strategy execution.

Building the Human-AI Team

The development of collaborative work environments is not devoid of challenges. The success of integrating AI within teams largely depends on building a culture that embraces innovation and change. This requires a shift in mindset where human workers view AI as a partner rather than a competitor.

Training programs that emphasize the strengths of AI and human capabilities can foster this mindset change. Moreover, organizations should encourage cross-disciplinary teams where individuals are exposed to various perspectives and approaches, blending technical prowess with creative insights.

For example, Google's initiative to integrate AI into its teams includes comprehensive training sessions that teach employees how to work alongside AI tools while empowering them to innovate. This approach has proven successful, leading to the development of groundbreaking products such as smart assistants and machine learning platforms that anticipate user needs before they are articulated.

Practical Application: The Tech Startup Model

To illustrate the tangible benefits of collaborative environments facilitated by AI, consider the tech startup sector, where lean operations require tight-knit collaboration and rapid innovation. Startups like Lemonade, a tech-driven insurance company, utilize an AI workforce in tandem with human teams. AI systems handle claims processing with impressive speed and accuracy, freeing human agents to focus on customer service and personalized advice.

The startup's ecosystem is a testament to an AI-driven collaborative model's effectiveness, blending machine efficiency with human empathy to deliver superior service and drive company growth. Such examples underscore the vitality of AI-enhanced collaboration, demonstrating how organizations can pivot and thrive in an innovation-centric landscape.

As we transition to the next subchapter, we explore how AI-driven transformations in work environments are redefining career pathways, emphasizing roles related to AI development, management, and ethics. This ongoing evolution demands adaptability and foresight from both individuals and organizations navigating the future of work.

Redefining Career Pathways in an AI-Driven World

In the rapidly evolving ecosystem of the modern workplace, the influence of artificial intelligence (AI) is undeniable. This transformation calls for a thorough reexamination of career pathways as AI becomes more embedded in diverse professional landscapes. The integration of AI into industries once relying heavily on human labor is presenting unprecedented opportunities and demanding new skills. As we navigate this dynamic environment, understanding how AI technology is reshaping careers is crucial for both individuals and organizations seeking to thrive in an era where machine and human co-create their future.

The discourse around AI often centers on the displacement of jobs, but what is less talked about is how AI is also creating new avenues and enriching existing roles. Careers are being redefined with each technological innovation, requiring a shift from traditional expectations. From AI development and programming to AI ethics and management, fresh opportunities abound, calling for professionals equipped with a distinct set of skills that encompass technical acumen and ethical insight.

The Emergence of New Roles

The advent of AI has led to the emergence of completely new career roles and paths, presenting vast opportunities for the workforce to expand into unprecedented territories. As AI systems become more sophisticated, the demand for specialists who can develop, maintain, and regulate these technologies is rising. Roles such as AI ethicists, data scientists, machine learning engineers, and AI trainers are becoming more prominent.

For example, consider the role of an AI ethicist. As AI systems become a staple across business operations, concerns about their ethical implications are at the forefront. Companies are now hiring AI ethicists to ensure that their AI deployments are aligned with ethical standards and societal norms. These professionals assess the potential biases in AI algorithms, analyze their social impact, and work to ensure the transparency and accountability of AI solutions.

Moreover, AI-related roles require continuous skill refinement and a willingness to adapt to technological advancements. This requires a workforce that is resilient, knowledgeable, and ready to engage with lifelong learning initiatives. Institutions offering specialized training programs tailored towards AI literacy and advanced technical skills are proliferating, providing an educational framework for these emerging careers.

Reskilling and Upskilling for the Future

Navigating a career in an AI-driven world demands an emphasis on reskilling and upskilling. For professionals in professions that were traditionally not technology-intensive, this transition involves embracing new competencies that allow them to work alongside AI or within AI-enhanced environments.

For instance, take the field of healthcare, where AI is making significant inroads in diagnostic processes. Medical professionals are now receiving training in how to interpret AI-generated insights to complement their assessments. Radiologists, for example, are using AI algorithms to enhance image analysis, improving diagnostic accuracy and efficiency. This shift requires medical professionals to be adept in AI-centric tools, augmenting their traditional training with new technological acumen.

Organizations, too, play a critical role in facilitating this transition for their workforce by investing in continuous education programs. They offer workshops, online courses, and certifications focused on AI technologies, ensuring that their employees are capable and confident in using AI tools to drive innovation.

Redefining Soft Skills in an AI World

The AI revolution not only demands new technical skills but also redefines the importance of soft skills. In roles increasingly automated by AI, human workers must leverage skills AI cannot replicate. Creativity, emotional intelligence, complex problem-solving, and ethical judgment are integral to co-creating with AI systems.

An illustrative case can be seen in customer service roles. AI chatbots are handling a growing number of routine interactions, but when complex issues arise, human workers are needed to navigate nuanced conversations requiring empathy and understanding. This scenario necessitates training programs that emphasize the development of these soft skills, ensuring workers can seamlessly transition to roles that make use of these uniquely human traits.

Moreover, professionals must develop strategic thinking and adaptability. As organizations continue to adapt AI systems, the ability to oversee these transitions with agility becomes invaluable. These skills foster a flexible mindset, preparing professionals to manage the unforeseen challenges and opportunities AI presents.

Education and Training Paradigms for an AI Era

The shift towards an AI-centric career landscape is prompting a reevaluation of educational paradigms. Universities and training institutes are reimagining their curricula to include AI literacy as a fundamental component. Beyond just the technical aspects of AI, educational programs are incorporating courses on AI ethics, human-AI interaction, and the societal impacts of AI technology.

Harnessing partnerships between academia and industry, educational institutions are creating dynamic environments for learning and innovation. Cooperative education models, internships, and research sabbaticals provide students with real-world opportunities to apply AI concepts, thereby reinforcing theoretical knowledge with practical experience.

Consider a university establishing a dedicated AI lab supported by industry leaders in technology. Students partake in interdisciplinary projects addressing real-world problems, gaining invaluable insights into the practical applications of AI. This approach not only prepares them for the technical challenges of tomorrow but also instills the confidence needed to spearhead innovation in their chosen fields.

Rethinking Career Trajectories

In an AI-driven world, career trajectories are no longer linear. The traditional notion of climbing a career ladder is giving way to more fluid career matrices, where diverse skills and experiences are prized over tenure or specific industry placements.

An enlightening example involves an individual beginning their career in marketing who then transitions into a role blending AI and digital analytics. As AI continues to revolutionize marketing strategies through personalized consumer insights, the marketer integrates AI-powered tools to design campaigns that resonate deeply with target audiences. This career transformation illustrates how AI enables professionals to pivot across industries, taking on hybrid roles that align with burgeoning technological trends.

Organizations further support their workforce by fostering an environment that values diverse talents and encourages interdisciplinary collaboration. Flexible work arrangements, mentorship programs, and networks of like-minded professionals support workers as they explore new career possibilities within the organization, ensuring sustained professional growth and fulfillment.

Practical Application: Navigating the AI Career Landscape

To comprehend how AI is redefining careers tangibly, let us examine a practical case study. Company X, a leader in the financial sector, sought to integrate AI into their operations to enhance efficiency and customer experiences. The decision to adopt AI required a workforce transformation strategy, focusing on reskilling their employees.

The company launched an in-house academy dedicated to AI training, offering courses spanning basic AI literacy to advanced AI programming. Employees across departments participated, applying their new knowledge directly to their roles. For example, the risk management team integrated AI algorithms into their assessments, improving their ability to predict financial risks effectively.

Furthermore, Company X hired AI specialists to develop custom AI tools tailored to their unique organizational needs, reinforcing the bond between technology and their core business functions. This immersive learning environment not only equipped employees with the necessary skills to excel in an AI-augmented job but also cultivated a culture of innovation and adaptive leadership.

Anchoring their strategy in continuous education, Company X set an example for how businesses can successfully support employees in transitioning to AI-enhanced roles. Employees, feeling empowered and valued, embraced their new responsibilities with enthusiasm and confidence, achieving higher productivity and job satisfaction.

In essence, this case study illustrates the transformative potential of synthesizing AI with existing business paradigms, showing how AI can lead to meaningful career growth and enrichment.

As we continue with our exploration in Chapter 7, understanding these transformative shifts in career pathways empowers readers to grasp the full spectrum of AI's impact on the workforce. With AI redefining roles and environments, individuals and organizations alike must embrace change, nurturing a workforce capable of co-creating a future where human ingenuity and technological prowess converge seamlessly.

As we conclude Chapter 7, it becomes clear that the intertwining of AI and human capability represents not only a shift in the workplace but a profound realignment in how we perceive and execute our roles in the modern economy. By redefining roles, enhancing skills, navigating job transitions, and fostering collaborative environments, AI offers us a panorama of possibilities, where human ingenuity and machine precision can coalesce to achieve unprecedented innovation.

The insights offered throughout these subchapters reflect the necessity for adaptability and resilience—attributes that are crucial as we journey deeper into an AI-empowered era. As we explored, the integration of AI accentuates the importance of creative and strategic capabilities, urging professionals to embrace continuous learning and revisit career pathways with a future-oriented mindset. The narrative demonstrates that while challenges persist, the potential for new, meaningful contributions within an AI-supported framework is vast and compelling.

As readers, we are encouraged to integrate these learnings into our personal and professional endeavors. The opportunity to co-create with machines is not a distant vision but a present reality, challenging us to harness these advancements responsibly and innovatively. In engaging with this transformative journey, we find ourselves equipped with a broader understanding to navigate and sculpt the future landscape of work.

Looking forward, our exploration does not halt at the workplace. In the chapters ahead, we will delve into the broader social, ethical, and technological implications of AI, questioning how these powerful tools can be aligned with human values and aspirations for the greater good. It's a continuation that promises to expand on how we can not only adapt to change but lead it toward a more promising tomorrow. Keep reading as we broach these profound discussions, setting the stage for thoughtful engagement and purposeful innovation.

CHAPTER 8: SOCIAL DYNAMICS AI AND HUMAN INTERACTION

I n an era where technology is an inseparable part of our daily lives, the convergence of artificial intelligence and social dynamics is revolutionizing the way we interact, communicate, and build communities. As we journey deeper into the digital age, it becomes crucial to understand how AI is not only reshaping individual interactions but also the broader societal constructs that define human connection. This chapter, Social Dynamics AI and Human Interaction, serves as a gateway to exploring the multifaceted roles AI plays in enhancing human relational capabilities.

We begin by delving into AI as a social facilitator, examining the sophisticated algorithms that power social networking platforms and AI-driven matchmaking services. In a world growing more connected yet paradoxically isolated, AI emerges as a key player in nurturing personal and professional bonds. This section sets the groundwork for grasping the technology's potential to foster a sense of community and belonging in the digital sphere.

From there, we transition to the evolving landscape of

communication, where AI's influence is nothing short of transformative. AI-driven advancements, ranging from language translation tools that dismantle linguistic barriers to virtual assistants that streamline communication, have redefined our interactions. This subchapter highlights how AI not only adapts to our communication needs but amplifies clarity and efficiency, paving the way for practical implementations that transcend traditional boundaries.

As we proceed, we confront the profound yet often subtle impact of AI on social behaviors. By scrutinizing AI-mediated interactions, we uncover technology's capacity to mold decision-making, social norms, and cultural trends. Through insightful case studies and interviews with experts, we provoke thought on the delicate balance between technology's influence and individual autonomy, pressing on the ethical considerations that accompany our evolving social fabric.

Building on these ideas, the subsequent section explores AI's role in constructing and sustaining communities. The potential of AI to promote inclusion and diversity, both online and offline, is immense. By spotlighting AI-powered platforms that drive civic engagement and collaborative problem-solving, we illustrate how human ingenuity, combined with machine efficiency, can drive meaningful social progress and foster communities centered around collective well-being.

Finally, we envision a future characterized by human-AI collaboration as the societal norm. This concluding subchapter synthesizes insights from prior discussions, offering a comprehensive framework for integrating AI into social structures. As we reflect on ethical considerations and the paramount importance of transparency, we present a vision for a collaborative society where AI enriches the human experience, facilitating deeper understanding and connection.

As we navigate through this chapter, the thematic strands

of community, communication, and collaboration intertwine to form a tapestry that reflects the transformative potential of AI in redefining social dynamics. By examining where we stand today and envisioning the future possibilities, we aim to equip readers with a nuanced understanding of the symbiotic relationship between humanity and technology, readying them for the book's broader exploration of AI-driven evolution.

AI as a Social Facilitator

In the digital age, connectivity has expanded beyond traditional human-to-human interactions, allowing technology to play a pivotal role in social dynamics. Artificial Intelligence (AI), as a key player in this transformation, emerges not merely as a tool but as an active facilitator of social interactions. The use of AI in fostering relationships, both personal and professional, has brought about a paradigm shift in how we network, communicate, and maintain social connections. In this subchapter, we delve into the core mechanics of AI as a social facilitator, illustrating its capabilities and the resultant enhancement of social ties.

The Technology Behind AI Social Facilitation

To understand AI's integral role in social facilitation, it is critical to dissect the technologies underpinning it. Predominantly, the landscape is shaped by advanced algorithms, machine learning models, and data analytics. AI-driven platforms utilize complex algorithms designed to process vast amounts of data and make connections that might not be immediately apparent to humans. These algorithms analyze user behaviors, preferences, and past interactions to suggest potential connections or provide recommendations for social engagement.

Social Networking Algorithms

Social networking platforms like Facebook, LinkedIn, and Twitter have long utilized AI to personalize and optimize user experiences. By analyzing user data, these platforms deliver content that is likely to resonate with individual users, thereby increasing engagement. AI identifies patterns in user interactions to recommend new connections, enhancing the likelihood of aligned interests and mutual benefits.

Consider LinkedIn's "People You May Know" feature. This AI-enabled tool systematically analyzes a user's profile, connections, and activity to suggest potential professional contacts. By leveraging machine learning, LinkedIn can predict who might be relevant to a user's career goals, helping to bridge gaps in their professional network.

AI-Driven Matchmaking Services

Matchmaking is another prominent area where AI excels as a social facilitator. Dating platforms like Tinder and OkCupid employ AI to match users based on compatibility scores determined by algorithms that assess users' interests, preferences, and online behavior. AI in these platforms ensures that users are matched with potential partners who align with their personal values and aspirations, increasing the likelihood of forming meaningful connections.

For example, eHarmony utilizes a robust AI framework that analyzes user data through comprehensive questionnaires. The platform's algorithms then match individuals based on psychological compatibility, enhancing the prospects of a successful relationship.

Expanding Professional Networks

AI is also instrumental in expanding professional networks, playing a crucial role in corporate and business interactions. AI-driven systems facilitate networking opportunities by matching professionals with similar interests, backgrounds, and career goals. Tools like Salesforce's Einstein and Microsoft's Cortana employ AI to identify potential collaborators and business opportunities, using data insights to guide companies in enhancing productivity and collaboration.

An interesting case study is that of a marketing consultancy firm that integrated AI into its client relationship management system. The AI analyzed clients' engagement patterns and suggested potential cross-industry partnerships based on their business activities. This approach not only widened the consultancy's professional network but also generated lucrative business opportunities through strategic alliances.

AI in Community Building

Beyond individual relationships, AI plays a significant role in fostering community and belonging. Platforms designed to cultivate communities leverage AI to ensure inclusivity, diversity, and active participation. Meetup is one such platform that utilizes AI to recommend events and groups based on users' interests and locations, promoting socialization and community engagement.

AI also aids in managing online communities by moderating content and interactions. It can identify and flag inappropriate or harmful content, ensuring community standards are maintained, creating a safer and more inclusive environment.

Practical Application: Real-World Case Study

Let's explore a practical application of AI as a social facilitator through the case study of Meetup's AI-powered recommendation engine. Meetup sought to increase user engagement and satisfaction by aligning user interests with relevant events and communities. The AI system was designed to analyze user profiles, past event attendance, feedback, and geographic preferences.

The AI periodically updated recommendations based on users' behavior changes, adapting to evolving interests. Consequently, users reported an increase in relevant event suggestions, leading to heightened engagement and community participation. Meetup's strategic use of AI not only enhanced its platform's user experience but also demonstrated the potential of AI in fostering social connections and community building.

As we've explored, AI's role as a social facilitator is profound, leveraging technology to nurture connections across personal, professional, and community domains. The subsequent subchapter will delve into the communication evolution in the age of AI, exploring how AI is not only transforming interactions but is also breaking new ground in language translation and virtual assistant technologies. By illuminating these aspects, we continue to unravel AI's expansive contribution to strengthening social networks and interaction dynamics.

Communication Evolution in the Age of AI

Communication has always been a vital component of human existence, serving as a bridge that connects individuals, cultures, and nations. As we traverse the complexities of the 21st century, the emergence of artificial intelligence (AI) presents a significant evolution in the way communication is conducted and experienced. This subchapter explores AI's transformative role in our communicative practices, emphasizing its ability to transcend traditional boundaries and customize interactions like never before.

Throughout history, each major technological advancement— from the invention of the telephone to the rise of the internet —has contributed to reshaping our communication landscape. Today, AI builds on these foundations, introducing capabilities that redefine and expand the possibilities of human interaction. By examining the tools and technologies at the heart of this transformation, we can gain a deeper understanding of AI's potential to enhance our communicative endeavors.

AI-Powered Language Translation

One of the most immediate and impactful contributions of AI to modern communication is its ability to break down language barriers. Language translation tools powered by AI, such as Google Translate and DeepL, utilize sophisticated machine learning algorithms to translate text and speech with high degrees of accuracy. These tools are continuously learning from vast datasets, enabling them to provide contextually accurate translations that capture nuances and idiomatic expressions.

Consider a global corporation conducting business across multiple countries. Linguistic diversity could present significant challenges to efficient communication. However, AI translation tools empower seamless and effective interactions between employees, clients, and partners, irrespective of the languages they speak. By facilitating clear and efficient communication, these tools not only streamline business operations but also foster a sense of global community.

In educational contexts, AI-driven translation technologies enable students from around the world to access learning materials in their native languages, democratizing education and broadening opportunities for knowledge acquisition. The ability to translate literary works, academic papers, and educational content in real-time holds promise for furthering cross-cultural understanding and collaboration.

Virtual Assistants as Communication Aides

AI-powered virtual assistants have become increasingly prevalent, serving as personal communication aides that optimize our daily interactions. From providing weather updates and scheduling appointments to sending emails and retrieving information, virtual assistants like Apple's Siri, Amazon's Alexa, and Google's Assistant have embedded themselves in the routines of millions of users worldwide.

Imagine waking up to a personalized morning briefing curated by your virtual assistant. This briefing, designed to match your interests and preferences, covers essential news updates, calendar appointments, and reminders, enabling you to prepare effectively for the day ahead. By streamlining these interactions, AI enhances productivity and personal organization, allowing individuals to focus on meaningful tasks that require human ingenuity.

In professional settings, virtual assistants can automate routine tasks, freeing up valuable time for employees to address more complex and strategic endeavors. For instance, an AI-driven virtual assistant can transcribe meeting notes, manage customer inquiries, and coordinate project timelines, removing roadblocks and enhancing workplace efficiency.

Adaptive Communication: Tailoring to User Needs

AI's ability to adapt communication to individual preferences stands as one of its most remarkable features. Unlike traditional one-size-fits-all communication methods, AI can personalize interactions based on user habits, behaviors, and context. This adaptive approach results in communication experiences that are not only efficient but also deeply resonant.

Take Customer Relationship Management (CRM) systems as an example. Equipped with AI capabilities, CRM platforms can analyze customer interactions, preferences, and feedback to create personalized communication strategies. By delivering messages aligned with customer needs and preferences, businesses foster stronger relationships, enhance customer satisfaction, and achieve higher retention rates.

Similarly, AI's adaptability finds applications in personalized healthcare, where virtual health assistants provide tailored advice and monitoring based on patient history and health data.

This customized communication empowers individuals to take proactive measures towards their health and well-being, leading to improved health outcomes.

Enhancing Accessibility through AI Communication Tools

The power of AI-driven communication extends to enhancing accessibility for individuals with disabilities. By breaking down barriers that traditionally hinder communication, AI creates inclusive environments where everyone can participate and contribute meaningfully.

Voice recognition technologies have played a pivotal role in assisting those with speech impairments. AI-powered applications convert spoken language into text, enabling individuals with speech disabilities to communicate effectively. Similarly, speech synthesis technologies offer benefits for those who are visually impaired, reading digital text aloud and enabling seamless integration into the digital world.

Moreover, AI facilitates the advancement of tools that support individuals with hearing impairments. Real-time transcription services and visual sign language recognition systems harness AI's capabilities to convert audio into readable text or sign language, ensuring that communication remains uninterrupted.

The Role of AI in Cultural Preservation

Beyond facilitating communication, AI plays an evolving role in preserving cultural heritage and languages at risk of extinction. Many societies are experiencing the erosion of their linguistic identities as global languages dominate. AI, however, offers a potential lifeline through the creation of digital archives and resources that preserve endangered languages and dialects.

Projects like Google's AI-driven language documentation efforts demonstrate the potential of technology to capture oral histories and cultural narratives, transforming them into accessible formats for future generations. By safeguarding intangible cultural heritage, these initiatives contribute to the richness of human diversity and foster greater cross-cultural understanding.

Practical Application: AI in Crisis Communication

One of the most striking examples of AI's transformative impact lies in its role during times of crisis. In emergency situations, timely and accurate communication can mean the difference between life and death. AI has demonstrated its potential to assist first responders and governments in delivering critical information to affected populations.

Consider the application of AI during natural disasters, such as hurricanes or earthquakes. By analyzing vast amounts of data from multiple sources, AI systems can detect patterns and predict developments, enabling authorities to issue warnings and evacuation notices efficiently. These AI-driven communication systems can translate messages into multiple languages, ensuring that all individuals, regardless of linguistic or cultural background, receive the necessary information to stay safe.

Similarly, AI-powered chatbots and automated hotline systems enable real-time, continuous communication with affected communities, providing updates, safety protocols, and avenues for assistance. By streamlining these communication channels, AI enhances emergency response efforts and contributes to disaster resilience.

Transitioning Forward

As we witness the profound ways AI is reshaping our communication landscape, it becomes evident that these technologies are poised to redefine social interaction paradigms for years to come. The adaptive capacities, accessibility benefits, and cultural preservation opportunities offered by

AI promise a future where communication is more inclusive, personalized, and efficient. However, as we explore AI's influence on communication, we must also examine the broader implications on human social behavior. Understanding how AI influences cultural norms and individual decision-making requires a deeper exploration of its subtle impact on the fabric of society. This investigation will be the focus of the next subchapter, delving into AI's intricate role in shaping social behaviors and cultural trends.

AI's Influence on Social Behaviors

As we navigate the complex landscape of social dynamics in the digital age, it is indispensable to scrutinize the subtle yet profound impact that artificial intelligence (AI) has on our social behaviors. AI technologies have woven themselves into the fabric of contemporary society, subtly influencing how we make decisions, adhere to social norms, and follow cultural trends. This subchapter delves into these influences and examines the ways AI is shaping, and sometimes reshaping, our societal attitudes and behaviors.

One of the most significant ways AI influences social behaviors is through the algorithms that govern social media platforms. These algorithms are designed to maintain user engagement by curating content tailored to individual preferences. However, these seemingly benign mechanisms can have unforeseen consequences. By consistently exposing users to similar types of content, algorithms can create echo chambers or filter bubbles where users are isolated from diverse perspectives. This can reinforce existing biases and social norms, making it harder for individuals to engage with differing viewpoints, ultimately affecting societal polarization.

Case Study: The Role of AI in Public Opinion Formation

Consider the 2016 U.S. Presidential election, where AI-driven algorithms played a pivotal role in disseminating information across social media. Studies have shown that content promoted by these algorithms affected public opinion by prioritizing sensational or biased information that drove engagement. These platforms' algorithmic decisions altered how many individuals perceived candidates and issues, subtly nudging public opinion in one direction or another. The role of AI in this scenario raises critical questions about the balance between allowing technology to manage information flow and preserving the richness of human discourse.

The Influence of AI on Social Norms

AI also plays a role in reinforcing or reshaping social norms. By observing patterns in human behavior, AI models can predict popular trends and influence how products and services are marketed. For instance, AI-driven trend analysis in the fashion industry offers insights into evolving consumer preferences, enabling companies to predict the next big trend. As consumers are increasingly influenced by AI-curated suggestions, these trends become self-reinforcing, subtly dictating social norms around style and identity.

AI's imprint on social norms extends to workplace behaviors as well. AI systems in professional environments can shape employee conduct by setting new standards for productivity and efficiency. Automated performance tracking tools encourage workers to align their behaviors with precision-focused AI measures, sometimes prioritizing productivity over creativity or innovation.

Cultural Trends and AI

In addition to influencing social norms, AI molds cultural trends. As AI tools become more sophisticated, they can influence the production and consumption of art, music, and literature. For example, AI algorithms are used to analyze and reproduce musical patterns, sometimes producing entirely new compositions. Musicians and artists are increasingly collaborating with AI to inspire novel artistic expressions that might not arise from human creativity alone.

Moreover, AI tools in film and media provide filmmakers with insights into audience preferences, influencing the types of narratives and characters that dominate screens. Streaming platforms utilize AI to recommend content based on viewing history, subtly guiding cultural consumption patterns and, in turn, broader cultural trends.

Impacts on Decision-Making

AI's role in decision-making can be both empowering and intrusive. Organizations use AI-driven data analysis to make strategic decisions, relying on machines to parse complex data and identify patterns that the human eye might miss. This enhances the decision-making process by providing comprehensive insights. However, the reliance on AI can raise concerns about the diminishing role of human intuition and experience in decision-making, potentially leading to decisions that lack a nuanced understanding of human context and ethics.

Practical Example: AI in Recruitment Processes

A practical example of AI's role in decision-making is its use in recruitment processes. AI algorithms screen resumes and rank candidates based on predefined criteria. While this streamlines the hiring process, it can also introduce biases if the data used to train the algorithms reflects historical biases. For instance, if a company's past hiring data shows a preference for candidates from certain demographic backgrounds, the AI might perpetuate these biases, challenging its impact on promoting an equitable workplace.

The Balance between Technology and Autonomy

The pervasive influence of AI presents challenges in balancing technology-driven influences with individual autonomy. While

AI can aid in making informed decisions, over-reliance on algorithmic outcomes can diminish personal agency. Individuals must cultivate a degree of skepticism and awareness to ensure they remain the primary agents of their decisions and social interactions.

As we reflect on the far-reaching implications of AI's influence on social behaviors, it's crucial to maintain a vigilant stance in assessing how these technologies shape not only our individual choices but also the collective consciousness. This subchapter underscores the need for ongoing dialogue between technologists, ethicists, and policymakers to navigate the gray areas of AI's social impact.

To solidify our understanding, let us examine a real-life scenario: the integration of AI into mental health applications. AI-powered apps offer tailored recommendations and therapies based on user data, enhancing accessibility to mental health resources. Yet, these very same technologies raise concerns about privacy and the depersonalized nature of AI-guided therapy. This contemporary application of AI illustrates the complexity of balancing technological benefits with mindful consideration of human needs and values.

As we transition our focus to the next subchapter, where we explore AI's role in building communities, we continue to unravel the intricate ways in which AI shapes our social fabric, encouraging us to remain active participants in this evolving narrative.

Building Communities with AI

As the digital landscape continues to evolve, the potential for artificial intelligence to build and sustain communities becomes increasingly significant. Unlike traditional methods of community-building, which rely heavily on human interaction and coordination, AI introduces novel tools and platforms capable of fostering inclusivity and diversity across various settings. This subchapter aims to explore these innovations, demonstrating how AI technologies serve as catalysts for civic engagement, collective problem-solving, and social good. We will delve into real-world examples of AI-facilitated community projects, highlighting the synergy between human ingenuity and machine efficiency.

The Current Landscape of AI in Community Building

Before diving into specific case studies, it's crucial to understand the backdrop against which AI operates in community building. Today, we observe a world where technology-mediated interactions are ubiquitous, with platforms like Facebook, LinkedIn, and Slack becoming essential tools for forming and maintaining community bonds. However, AI's role in this landscape is distinctly different from that of traditional social networks. Where algorithms associated with these platforms once passively connected people based on loose associations, AI actively curates experiences to foster genuine connections and collaborations.

Take, for instance, Meetup, a platform that utilizes AI algorithms to suggest events and groups that align with users' interests and previous activities. Through machine learning, the platform refines its understanding of individual preferences over time, enhancing its recommendations and facilitating meaningful engagements among users who may have otherwise never crossed paths. By continuously adapting and optimizing user suggestions, AI transforms simple meetings into thriving interactive communities.

AI Tools for Inclusivity and Diversity

One of AI's most powerful contributions to community building lies in its ability to promote inclusivity and diversity. With AI tools, communities can transcend geographical, cultural, and linguistic boundaries, enabling diverse groups of people to unite around shared goals and interests.

A compelling example is AI-driven translation services, such as Google's AI-powered translation tools. These services enable seamless communication across language barriers within international communities, offering real-time translations that preserve the nuances of human conversation. In virtual spaces like global forums or multinational organizations, AI-driven translation empowers individuals from different linguistic backgrounds to communicate effectively and participate equally, fostering inclusivity and reducing the friction that often accompanies cross-cultural interactions.

Beyond language, AI tools can also be leveraged to analyze demographic data and optimize content distribution to ensure diverse representation within community platforms. For example, online forums and social media platforms increasingly rely on AI to detect and mitigate biases, ensuring that all users experience equitable treatment and access. AI can flag and filter inappropriate comments or discriminatory language, helping to create a safe environment where everyone feels valued and respected.

Case Study: Improving Civic Engagement with AI

The power of AI in fostering civic engagement is evident in various community-driven initiatives. Consider the case study of "Neighborly," an AI-powered platform designed to boost civic engagement within local communities. By harnessing natural language processing and predictive analytics, Neighborly identifies pressing issues within neighborhoods and connects residents with opportunities to address them collectively.

Operating much like a social media feed, Neighborly aggregates local news, events, and discussions. Its AI algorithms then analyze these data points to identify patterns and trends. For instance, if the majority of residents express concern over traffic safety, the platform can suggest community meetings or discussions with local officials to tackle the issue head-on.

One of the most notable successes of Neighborly was its role in organizing a city-wide initiative in Portland, Oregon. Residents had voiced concerns about increasing traffic congestion and pedestrian safety in their neighborhoods. Leveraging its analytical capabilities, Neighborly facilitated a series of online town halls and strategy sessions where community members, local government, and urban planners collaborated. Together, they devised actionable solutions, such as implementing additional crosswalks and launching a public awareness campaign. By driving civic engagement through AI, Neighborly empowered the Portland community to enact tangible changes that improved the local quality of life.

AI's Role in Collective Problem-Solving

Collective problem-solving is another realm where AI's impact is transformative. When communities face shared challenges, AI can drive collaborative efforts by synthesizing large volumes of data and providing insights that inform decision-making processes.

A real-world illustration of AI's potential in this field is "Zooniverse," an online platform that uses citizen science to address various global challenges. Zooniverse harnesses AI to analyze data contributions from volunteers worldwide, accelerating the pace of research across disciplines ranging from ecology to astronomy.

In one specific project within the Zooniverse platform, researchers sought help in mapping the surface of Mars. Traditional methods would have involved extensive manpower and years of analysis. However, by employing AI algorithms to process and interpret images sent by satellites, Zooniverse was able to engage millions of volunteers in helping to identify and categorize surface features. Volunteers contributed their insights while the AI validated and aggregated these data points, resulting in the creation of comprehensive maps at unprecedented speed. This collaborative effort demonstrated how AI and community participation can harmoniously converge to solve complex problems while advancing scientific knowledge.

AI and Social Good: The Path Forward

While the potential for AI to build and sustain communities is vast, its success in driving social good is contingent upon mindful implementation. Any tools or platforms developed with AI must prioritize ethics, privacy, and transparency, ensuring that they address genuine community needs without compromising individual rights. This includes addressing concerns around data privacy, algorithmic biases, and the overall impact of AI on societal structures.

To illustrate, consider the example of "Civic Tech," a term referring to technology that enhances citizen-government interaction and engagement. Many Civic Tech initiatives employ AI to streamline processes like voting, public feedback, and resource allocation. However, they also face unique challenges, such as ensuring the security and privacy of sensitive data collected from citizens. To mitigate these challenges, successful projects often incorporate rigorous ethical frameworks that prioritize transparency and facilitate continuous community input.

As AI continues to evolve, it holds remarkable potential to redefine how we conceive of community and collaboration. The possibilities are endless—from optimizing local resource allocation and promoting sustainable tourism to facilitating education and healthcare access in underserved areas. By embracing AI's capabilities within community-building initiatives and aligning them with ethical best practices, we can drive meaningful societal progress.

Practical Application: Transforming Volunteerism with AI

To put this into perspective, let's examine the innovative application of AI in the realm of volunteerism. The platform "AI4Good," an initiative seeking to connect skilled volunteers with community projects worldwide, underscores AI's transformative potential.

AI4Good's algorithms match volunteers' skills with mission-driven projects that require specific expertise, ranging from web development and graphic design to humanitarian aid and environmental conservation. Volunteers simply input their skills, availability, and geographic preferences, allowing the AI to seamlessly pair them with suitable projects. This precision matching optimizes volunteer satisfaction and task efficiency, ensuring that resources are deployed where they can generate the maximum impact.

The success stories are abundant. In one standout example, AI4Good connected software developers with a nonprofit dedicated to wildlife conservation. The volunteers helped design a mobile application that tracks endangered species' movements, providing conservationists with real-time data and insights. This collaborative project not only amplified the nonprofit's reach but also empowered skilled individuals to contribute to global causes despite geographical constraints.

As AI reshapes the landscape of volunteerism, this approach exemplifies how technology can facilitate valuable connections while driving community-centric accomplishments.

As we transition into the next subchapter, we will explore the broader implications of human-AI collaboration within society. By understanding AI's role in community-building contexts, we lay the groundwork for envisioning a future where collective human-AI efforts enhance societal structures and foster inclusive, thriving communities.

Toward a Collaborative

As technology continues to evolve at an unprecedented pace, the prospect of a collaborative human-AI society is no longer a distant future but a burgeoning reality. The intersection of human intelligence and artificial intelligence presents a unique opportunity to engineer a world where these entities not only coexist but thrive together, enhancing humanity's potential in profound ways. In this subchapter, we will explore the frameworks required for integrating AI into social structures and emphasize the ethical considerations crucial to this integration. Through practical examples and real-life scenarios, we will illustrate how a collaborative human-AI society can drive positive change and promote a deeper understanding among individuals and communities.

The foundation of a collaborative human-AI society hinges on several key elements: transparency, ethical integrity, adaptability, and shared objectives. Transparency in AI operations is of paramount importance to build trust among users. Consider AI systems designed to assist in healthcare settings. These systems must be clear about how they make decisions regarding patient care. For instance, an AI-driven diagnostic tool should provide insights into how it analyzes patient data and reaches conclusions, ensuring that healthcare professionals and patients understand the rationale behind its recommendations. Such transparency not only fosters trust but also facilitates more informed decision-making, leading to improved patient outcomes.

Ethical considerations play a pivotal role in the integration of AI into social structures. As AI systems become more pervasive, they are increasingly involved in decisions that carry ethical implications. Take, for example, AI in recruitment processes, where algorithms are used to shortlist job candidates. Ensuring that these systems are free from bias and discrimination is critical to maintaining fairness and equality. This demands rigorous oversight and continuous evaluation of AI models to prevent unintended consequences that could perpetuate societal inequalities. By embedding ethical principles into the core design and operation of AI systems, we pave the way for a society that values human dignity and fosters inclusive growth.

Adaptability is another essential component of a collaborative human-AI society. The fast-evolving nature of technology calls for AI systems that can adapt to changing needs and contexts. In educational environments, for instance, AI-driven personalized learning platforms can revolutionize the way students engage with content. These platforms assess individual learning styles and pace, delivering customized educational experiences. By adapting to the unique needs of each student, AI can enhance learning outcomes and prepare future generations with the skills needed to navigate a tech-driven world.

Shared objectives between humans and AI systems are pivotal to realizing the full potential of a collaborative society. One of the most promising areas of application is in environmental conservation efforts. AI can analyze vast datasets to monitor environmental changes, predict natural disasters, and assist in conservation strategies. By aligning AI capabilities with human goals for environmental stewardship, we can foster sustainable practices and safeguard natural resources for future generations.

A practical example of how a collaborative human-AI society can manifest is the concept of "smart cities." These urban areas leverage AI technologies to manage resources efficiently, optimize traffic flow, reduce energy consumption, and enhance public safety. In such environments, AI systems work alongside human decision-makers to address urban challenges, improving the quality of life for residents. For instance, AI can analyze traffic patterns to optimize signal timings, reducing congestion and minimizing carbon emissions. Smart cities exemplify how human-AI collaboration can lead to innovative solutions that benefit society at large.

Real-life case studies further illustrate the potential of collaborative intelligence in action. One compelling example is the partnership between AI researchers and healthcare providers to tackle the challenge of early disease detection. By deploying AI algorithms that can process massive volumes of medical imaging data, researchers are improving the accuracy of early diagnoses. In cases such as breast cancer detection, AI systems have been shown to identify potential abnormalities with greater precision than human radiologists alone. This collaboration not only enhances diagnostic capabilities but also underscores the power of combining human expertise with AI advancements to achieve superior outcomes.

Another notable case study is the development of AI-driven platforms in the agricultural sector to address food security challenges. By providing farmers with data-driven insights into weather patterns, soil conditions, and crop health, AI systems enable more precise and sustainable agricultural practices. This collaboration empowers farmers to make informed decisions that enhance crop yield and quality while minimizing environmental impact. As a result, AI contributes to global efforts to reduce hunger and promote food sustainability, exemplifying how technology can be harnessed for social good.

The journey toward a collaborative human-AI society is not without its challenges, but with a commitment to ethical integrity, transparency, and shared vision, it holds the potential to redefine the way we interact with technology. The insights from this subchapter should serve as a precursor to exploring the broader ethical and governance frameworks necessary for ensuring that AI technologies are deployed responsibly and equitably. As we prepare to delve into these discussions, it is crucial to recognize the transformative power of human-AI collaboration in shaping a future that enhances human connections, promotes understanding, and enriches social experiences at every level.

In conclusion, the promise of a collaborative human-AI society lies not only in the technological advances that it encompasses but also in the opportunities it presents for building a more inclusive and equitable world. By embracing the principles outlined in this subchapter, we can lay the groundwork for a future where technology serves as a conduit for human advancement, creativity, and social progress.

As we reach the conclusion of Chapter 8, Social Dynamics — AI and Human Interaction, we find ourselves at the crossroads of technology and humanity. Throughout this chapter, we have meticulously explored the ways AI serves as a powerful social facilitator, transforming the fabric of human connections. From the algorithms that bridge personal and professional networks to the communication tools breaking down linguistic and informational barriers, AI is redefining how we interact and engage with one another.

We delved into how AI subtly influences social behaviors, shaping societal norms and cultural trends with profound implications for decision-making and personal autonomy. Our journey took us through diverse communities where AI acts as a beacon of inclusivity and collective growth, showcasing the incredible synergy between human creativity and machine efficiency. Finally, we envisioned a future where collaborative human-AI societies thrive, characterized by ethical integration and transparency.

The insights from this chapter offer a compelling blueprint for embracing AI's potential to enhance our social dynamics.

Whether you are a leader envisioning organizational growth, a communicator seeking clarity, or an individual navigating the complex landscape of digital interactions, the lessons learned here inspire us to harness AI's capabilities wisely.

As we transition to the forthcoming discussions on ethics and governance, the stage is set for a deeper exploration of AI's role as a collaborative partner in our societal evolution. Prepare to dive into the climactic analysis of collaborative intelligence, where human and machine potential coalesce to unlock new dimensions of innovation and understanding. Let this be your launching point into a future where AI not only complements but enriches the human experience, encouraging you to pursue this transformative journey with renewed curiosity and purpose.

CHAPTER 9: ETHICS AND GOVERNANCE NAVIGATING THE AI LANDSCAPE

As we stand at the threshold of an era defined by artificial intelligence, the profound challenges posed by this transformative technology command our immediate attention. Chapter 9, Ethics and Governance: Navigating the AI Landscape, embarks on a crucial exploration of the moral and regulatory dimensions that not only guide the development of AI technologies but determine their role in our shared future. This chapter delves deep into the ethical imperatives and governance frameworks that are essential for ensuring AI remains a force for good, fostering innovation while safeguarding humanity's core values.

Artificial intelligence holds immense potential to reshape industries, enhance productivity, and redefine the boundaries of human capability. However, along with these opportunities come significant ethical concerns. In Subchapter 1, The Ethical Imperative in AI Development, we explore the fundamental principles driving ethical decision-making in AI creation. This segment sets the stage by voicing the need for AI to align with human values and the moral duties of those who design and deploy these systems. Through real-world dilemmas and historical contexts, we underscore the risks of sidelining ethical considerations and emphasize the consequences of such oversight.

Trust and reliability stand at the heart of public acceptance of AI technologies. Subchapter 2, Transparency and Accountability in AI Systems, examines how transparency builds trust among stakeholders. It reveals mechanisms and practices that enable openness in AI operations and establishes accountability measures to ensure systems function as intended. This section empowers readers with insights into how leading organizations implement these principles, thereby enhancing the reliability and acceptance of their AI systems.

The third subchapter, Navigating Privacy and Data Security Concerns, shifts focus towards the intricate balance between technological progress and protecting individual privacy. As AI systems depend heavily on vast datasets, it becomes imperative to protect personal information vigilantly. We explore the complexities of global data flows and the strategies necessary for safeguarding privacy in this interconnected era, setting the foundation for secure and ethical AI practices.

Having established ethical and operational standards, we turn our attention to the underlying structures that guide AI development. Subchapter 4, Governance Frameworks for Ethical AI, investigates the policies and regulations shaping responsible AI use. Through a comparative analysis of governance models worldwide, this section distills effective strategies for societal integration of AI technologies, underscoring the need for continuous adaptation in response to technological evolution.

Finally, Subchapter 5, Cultivating a Collaborative Approach to AI Governance, advocates for multi-stakeholder involvement, advocating for diverse contributions in crafting comprehensive AI policies. Here, we examine how collaboration among technologists, ethicists, policymakers, and the public fosters a shared understanding and consensus-building in forging ethical AI practices. The chapter culminates in a call to action, inviting readers to engage proactively in shaping AI systems that prioritize human welfare and uphold democratic values.

Through this exploration, Chapter 9 provides a robust framework for thoughtful engagement with AI technologies, positioning ethics and governance as pivotal elements in navigating the AI landscape. It not only informs but inspires a collective journey towards an intelligent future aligned with human dignity and societal advancement.

The Ethical Imperative in AI Development

In our rapidly advancing digital age, the development and deployment of Artificial Intelligence (AI) are revolutionizing multiple facets of human life, from healthcare and education to transport and entertainment. However, as AI technologies increasingly permeate our daily lives, the imperative to embed ethical principles within their framework has become more pronounced than ever. The focus of this subchapter is on the necessity of aligning AI systems with human values and the moral imperatives that guide the creators and users of these technologies. By delving into real-world dilemmas, historical examples, and ethical quandaries, it underscores the critical importance of establishing robust ethical standards to ensure the sustainable and responsible growth of AI technologies.

The Foundations of Ethical AI

Ethics in AI development is not merely a theoretical concern but a practical necessity. The ethical foundations of AI are built on three core principles: responsibility, fairness, and transparency.

Firstly, responsibility entails that AI creators and operators are accountable for the actions and outcomes generated by AI systems. This means designing AI in ways that anticipate and mitigate negative impacts. For example, companies deploying AI in recruitment processes must ensure that their algorithms do not propagate existing biases in hiring practices.

Fairness, the second pillar, demands that AI technologies serve all societal segments equitably without favoring any group based on race, gender, or socioeconomic status. A historical lesson can be derived from the deployment of early face recognition systems, which showed considerable bias against certain racial groups. Such biases, if unchecked, could lead to broader social and legal ramifications, highlighting the need for rigorous testing and inclusive design processes.

Transparency, the third component, ensures that the operations and decisions made by AI systems are clear and understandable to its users. Without transparency, users cannot trust AI systems, and accountability becomes difficult to establish. As a practical step, companies like Google have implemented extensive documentation protocols for their AI systems to allow for user understanding and trust building.

Real-World Ethical Dilemmas

One of the most illustrative real-world dilemmas in AI development is seen in autonomous vehicles. These technologies must make split-second decisions that could have life-or-death consequences. The ethical imperative here is designing these systems to reflect societal values about life preservation and risk assessment. For instance, if an autonomous vehicle finds itself in a situation where a collision is inevitable, whether it should prioritize the safety of its passengers or the pedestrians outside is a profound ethical issue. Such dilemmas stress the need for establishing broad-based ethical standards and agree-upon norms in AI development.

Another pertinent case is in healthcare, where AI systems have been increasingly used for diagnosing diseases or recommending patient treatments. The ethical challenges are twofold; firstly, there is an imperative to ensure that the AI systems are accurately trained on diverse datasets to avoid medical misdiagnoses. Secondly, they must respect patient privacy and confidentiality, demanding developers to engage with these ethical considerations proactively.

The Role of Ethical Frameworks and Guidelines

Ethical AI development is guided by several frameworks and guidelines developed by organizations worldwide. The European Union's Ethics Guidelines for Trustworthy AI, for instance, outlines principles for human agency and oversight, technical robustness, and societal well-being. These guidelines serve as blueprints for companies and governments aiming to establish AI systems that are aligned with human values.

Case studies such as IBM's trusted AI initiatives demonstrate how companies can implement these principles effectively. IBM has put efforts into ensuring their AI systems have fairness, interpretability, and accountability, setting industry standards. By developing tools that assess the fairness and bias of their AI systems, they provide a model for responsibly deploying AI in commercial applications.

Moral Responsibilities of AI Creators and Users

Both creators and users of AI have distinctive moral responsibilities that must be considered to ensure ethical compliance. AI developers have to generate systems that respect user rights, emphasizing privacy and security while minimizing harm. They are tasked with foreseeing potential misuses and implementing safeguards against them.

On the user side, individuals and organizations using AI must be informed about the capabilities and limitations of the technology. Ethical usage demands comprehension of the implicit biases that AI technologies might carry and advocating for transparency in every AI system interaction. A practical scenario can be seen in content moderation on social media platforms, where AI tools are employed. Users must understand how these tools operate and develop strategies to handle the biases that might arise, ensuring that discussions about censorship and free speech are well-informed and balanced.

Historical Precendents and Current Initiatives

Historically, parallels can be drawn from the early era of the internet when privacy concerns and data security were initially overshadowed by the excitement of connectivity. Over time, industries and regulators recognized that ethical considerations were not supplementary but foundational to sustainable growth.

Currently, there are numerous initiatives promoting ethical AI. The Partnership on AI, a multi-stakeholder organization, aims to create best practices for AI technologies. Their approach encapsulates a collective responsibility model where various stakeholders, from academia to private sectors, collaborate to address AI's societal impacts.

Practical Case Study: AI in Criminal Justice

The criminal justice system provides a compelling case study for examining ethical AI development. AI algorithms are used to predict recidivism rates and other risk assessments. However, the use of such technologies has raised significant ethical concerns, particularly regarding bias against minorities, leading to calls for enhanced transparency and accountability measures.

For instance, studies have found that certain predictive policing algorithms can disproportionately target minority communities due to biased training data. To address these challenges, city governments and AI developers are working together to revise and monitor these algorithms, encouraging community-led oversight and transparency practices that can improve trust and efficacy.

By thoroughly examining these foundational principles and applying them across various industries, the ethical imperative in AI development fosters a landscape where technological innovations can thrive while resiliently woven into the fabric of societal norms and human values. Transitioning into the next subchapter, we will delve deeper into the interconnected principles of transparency and accountability, exploring how they underpin ethical governance in AI systems and help build an environment of trust and reliability.

Transparency and Accountability in AI Systems

In the rapidly advancing field of artificial intelligence (AI), two of the most debated and crucial aspects for ethical governance are transparency and accountability. As technology increasingly becomes integral to daily life and business operations, ensuring these elements are foundational to AI systems cannot be overstated. Transparency invites trust, while accountability ensures reliability. Together, they enable a robust framework for ethical AI development and deployment that serves the interests of both users and creators.

Understanding Transparency in AI

Transparency in AI refers to the openness of AI systems about how they function and make decisions. This encompasses the methodologies, algorithms, datasets, and decision-making criteria involved in AI processes. Transparency is imperative for several reasons. Firstly, it fosters trust among users, stakeholders, and society at large. When the mechanisms of AI systems are visible and comprehensible, users are more likely to trust the technology, understanding how outcomes are derived and what influences these processes.

Moreover, transparency provides insight into AI's internal workings, helping identify potential biases and errors in machine learning models. For example, if an AI system used for hiring decisions perpetuates gender or racial biases, knowing the datasets and criteria it employs is crucial to addressing and correcting these biases. Notably, the European Union's General Data Protection Regulation (GDPR) has highlighted transparency as a legal obligation, requiring that individuals have the right to understand the logic behind automated decisions.

However, achieving transparency in AI is not without its challenges. The complexity of many AI systems, particularly those using deep learning, often results in a "black box" effect, where the decision-making processes are difficult to interpret, even for their creators. While strides in explainable AI (XAI) aim to make these systems more understandable, balancing transparency with intellectual property rights and proprietary technology concerns remains a delicate task.

To illustrate the importance of transparency, consider the case of COMPAS, a risk assessment tool used in the U.S. judicial system to predict the likelihood of a criminal reoffending. When studies revealed that COMPAS was potentially biased against African American defendants, the lack of transparency in its algorithm came under scrutiny. This case underscored the necessity for open, interpretable systems, especially in critical applications like criminal justice, where bias can have severe human implications.

The Pillars of Accountability in AI

Accountability in AI is about establishing systems and structures that ensure AI operates as intended and provides clear channels for redress should issues arise. An accountable AI system is one where creators, operators, and users can identify who is responsible for the actions and outcomes of AI deployments. This is essential for rectifying faults, addressing biases, and ensuring that AI benefits society equitably.

To achieve accountability, organizations must implement comprehensive governance policies and regulatory compliance strategies. They need to define responsibility at every stage of AI development—from data collection and algorithm design to deployment and monitoring. This involves documenting decisions, maintaining logs of AI interactions, and providing audit trails that can be reviewed by external stakeholders when necessary.

One practical example of accountability is seen in the financial services industry, where AI systems are increasingly used for functions such as fraud detection and credit scoring. Financial institutions are required to adhere to strict regulations that demand not only transparency in the decision-making processes but also accountability should those decisions be flawed or discriminatory. In cases of error, such as unjust credit denial caused by an AI system, having rigid accountability measures allows companies to track the source of the error, correct it, and offer remedies to affected individuals.

Implementing Transparency and Accountability: Strategies and Best Practices

To successfully implement transparency and accountability, organizations must adopt a multi-faceted approach. Here are some strategies and best practices:

1. Engage in Continuous Monitoring and Evaluation: Regularly assess AI systems to ensure they function as expected and remain aligned with ethical guidelines. This involves ongoing monitoring and evaluation, employing both technical audits and human oversight.

2. Adopt Explainable AI Techniques: Use methods that make

AI decisions interpretable. Techniques like decision trees, rule-based systems, or surrogate models can be employed to provide clear rationales for AI decisions, enhancing understandability without compromising performance.

3. Establish Clear Documentation and Reporting Standards: Maintain comprehensive records of AI processes, decision criteria, and changes in algorithms or datasets. This documentation is essential for accountability, allowing stakeholders to understand the decision-making history and evolution of AI systems.

4. Foster Stakeholder Involvement: Include diverse groups in the AI development process to identify potential biases and ethical concerns. This could involve ethicists, sociologists, domain experts, and the communities impacted by AI decisions.

5. Implement a Governance Framework with Well-Defined Roles: Develop a governance structure that clearly outlines roles and responsibilities, ensuring there are designated individuals or teams accountable for every aspect of the AI lifecycle.

6. Create Feedback Mechanisms: Implement channels for users and affected individuals to provide feedback or report issues with AI systems. This could be through helpdesks, online forms, or dedicated support teams, ensuring accountability measures are responsive and user-centered.

Real-World Application: The Case of Algorithmic Transparency at Google

A compelling example of transparency and accountability in action is Google's approach to its AI systems. Google has initiated several measures to enhance transparency within its operations. One significant initiative is their AI Principles, which explicitly states that Google AI and its derivatives should be socially beneficial, avoid creating or reinforcing unfair bias, and be designed for interpretability. Google has also invested in explainable AI tools that aim to make their AI decisions more understandable to the public.

In practice, Google's commitment has been tested during instances such as their AI-powered search algorithms or YouTube's recommendation engine, where biases or content issues have arisen. Each situation prompts audits and refinements based on stakeholder feedback, demonstrating an ongoing commitment to transparency and accountability, which has improved user trust and adherence to ethical standards.

In conclusion, transparency and accountability are not mere ethical add-ons in the AI landscape but are essential components to building trust and ensuring AI grows in a way that is beneficial to society. As we advance into the subsequent sections, it becomes increasingly clear how these elements interplay with other facets of AI governance, ultimately influencing the global framework within which AI operates. With these foundations in place, we now turn our attention to the intricate dynamics of privacy and data security in the AI ecosystem, exploring how these aspects are managed and protected in a digital world.

Navigating Privacy and Data Security Concerns

In today's digital landscape, artificial intelligence is a powerful tool shaping industries and society. However, as AI systems continue to evolve, the question of privacy and data security becomes a critical issue, demanding both attention and ingenuity. The integration of AI into daily life has undoubtedly spurred significant advancements, but it has also sparked a vigilant discourse around safeguarding individual privacy rights within this new frontier. This subchapter explores the multi-faceted relationship between privacy, data security, and

AI innovation. It delves into the strategies necessary to balance technological growth with the ethical obligation to protect personal information.

The Essential Role of Data in AI Development

At the heart of AI's functionality is data. AI systems depend heavily on large datasets to learn, adapt, and make predictions. This data, often extracted from consumer behaviors, social media interactions, online searches, and more, underpins the algorithmic models that drive AI technologies. The volume and velocity at which data is collected are staggering, leading to immense opportunities and equally immense risks concerning privacy breaches and data misuse.

Consider the case of facial recognition technology. Law enforcement agencies employ AI-driven facial recognition tools, using vast photograph libraries to identify suspects or missing persons efficiently. While this has enhanced public safety measures, it has raised serious privacy concerns. Critics argue that such surveillance systems may violate personal privacy, as individuals find themselves being monitored without explicit consent. This exemplifies the ethical tension between harnessing technology's potential and preserving civil liberties.

Balancing Innovation with Privacy Rights

The challenge lies in enabling AI advancements without compromising fundamental rights to privacy. As AI systems process and analyze data at unprecedented scales, the safeguards placed around this information must be robust and proactive.

Anonymization techniques stand as a primary method to ensure privacy. By stripping datasets of identifiable information, organizations reduce the risk of exposing personal details if a breach occurs. Netflix's release of its dataset for a recommendation algorithm competition serves as a pertinent example. Though the data was anonymized, individuals were later re-identified, shedding light on the complexity of true anonymization and the need for continued innovation in privacy-preserving methods.

Consent remains another cornerstone of responsible data handling. Engaging users in transparent dialogues about how their data is used empowers them to make informed decisions regarding their privacy. The introduction of the European Union's General Data Protection Regulation (GDPR) in 2018 crystallized this approach, mandating that users be fully informed and participate actively in decisions regarding their personal data. The GDPR has set a global precedent in data privacy that organizations are increasingly adopting as a benchmark for their operations.

Security Measures for Data Protection

Alongside privacy, data security is crucial for ensuring that AI operates within ethical boundaries. Organizations must implement multi-layered security strategies to fend off cyber threats and unauthorized data access. Encryption, access controls, and regular security audits are fundamental practices that bolster data defenses. Encryption transforms data into a secure format, accessible only by authorized users, thus safeguarding sensitive information from unauthorized interception.

Consider the healthcare sector, where AI tools analyze patient data to improve diagnostic accuracy. With the stakes so high, data breaches can be catastrophic. The 2015 Anthem data breach, where hackers accessed over 78 million records, underscores the importance of rigorous data protection strategies. Post-breach, Anthem adopted sophisticated data encryption measures and regular risk assessments to fortify its defenses, demonstrating the necessity of adaptable security protocols in safeguarding sensitive information.

Navigating Cross-Border Data Challenges

AI's global reach introduces additional complexity concerning cross-border data flows. With data moving seamlessly across international boundaries, differing legal frameworks can create ambiguities and vulnerabilities in data protection. This necessitates a unified approach to privacy laws and regulations, facilitating secure and ethical AI operation in a globalized ecosystem.

The United States and the European Union, for instance, have recognized the need for harmonized data protection practices. Initiatives like the now-defunct EU-US Privacy Shield sought to bridge regulatory differences, though its invalidation by the European Court illustrates the ongoing challenge of creating universally accepted data protection agreements. The evolving nature of AI technology demands that such regulatory frameworks remain dynamic, allowing for rapid adaptations in response to new technological developments.

Case Study: Apple's Approach to Privacy

Apple Inc. presents a compelling illustration of how companies can balance innovation with privacy through comprehensive data security strategies. Known for its strong stance on user privacy, Apple integrates privacy features directly into its systems. Apple's differential privacy approach exemplifies anonymization techniques, allowing the company to glean valuable insights while safeguarding individual privacy.

In practice, differential privacy introduces random noise into datasets, preserving the data's usability without compromising personal information. This method enables Apple to refine its products and services without infringing on user privacy, highlighting the company's commitment to ethical innovation.

Furthermore, Apple enforces end-to-end encryption across its platforms, ensuring that data is scrambled on users' devices and can only be decrypted by them. This means that even if data is intercepted, it remains unreadable without the appropriate decryption key, providing an enhanced level of security.

By prioritizing and investing in privacy technologies and transparent user policies, Apple has set an industry standard for data protection, demonstrating how companies can navigate the delicate balance between innovation and privacy respect.

In conclusion, maintaining trust in AI systems hinges on our ability to protect privacy and ensure data security. As we advance into a future where AI systems are not just ubiquitous but deeply entwined with our daily lives, the imperative to create safe, secure, and privacy-conscious AI systems becomes even more critical. As we move towards the next subchapter, we will explore the governance frameworks that play an essential role in maintaining this delicate balance, ensuring that AI not only enhances our capabilities but does so with respect and consideration for our rights.

Governance Frameworks
for Ethical AI

As we move further into the 21st century, artificial intelligence continues to evolve at breakneck speed. The rapid advancements bring about a profound need for structured governance frameworks to ensure ethical and responsible deployment. This subchapter explores the various layers of governance frameworks necessary for steering AI development and use towards societal good. As we do so, we highlight the significance of international agreements, government regulations, and industry standards in shaping practices that prioritize ethical considerations.

The term "governance frameworks" encompasses formal and informal structures, policies, and processes that guide the development and use of AI. These frameworks are designed to align AI technologies with societal values and ensure that their impact is beneficial, equitable, and fair. More than a mere regulatory function, these frameworks serve as a foundation for trust in AI, fostering an ecosystem where innovation can thrive while maintaining public confidence.

The Role of International Agreements and Conventions

In an increasingly connected world, the influence of international agreements in shaping AI governance is undeniable. Organizations such as the United Nations and the European Union have been at the forefront of developing AI ethics guidelines that reflect a consensus on fundamental principles. The OECD Principles on AI, for example, provide a clear direction for AI development, emphasizing inclusivity, transparency, and accountability. These principles encourage nations to incorporate ethical standards into their own governance strategies, thereby ensuring a level of consistency and cooperation across borders.

A notable example is the EU's General Data Protection Regulation (GDPR), which has become a gold standard for privacy and data protection worldwide. Although primarily focused on privacy, it indirectly impacts AI development by setting stringent requirements for data handling, thereby influencing how AI systems collect, store, and process information. Countries worldwide have either adopted similar regulations or adapted their existing frameworks to be compliant with these international standards, underscoring the importance of global cooperation in AI governance.

Government Regulations: Balancing Innovation and Ethics

At a national level, governments play a critical role in crafting regulations that ensure AI technologies are ethical, safe, and aligned with public interests. The challenge lies in balancing the dual objectives of promoting technological innovation and safeguarding societal values. Regulations need to be flexible enough to accommodate AI's dynamic growth, yet stringent enough to prevent harm or misuse.

One approach governments have taken is the creation of statutory bodies or commissions dedicated to overseeing AI ethics and governance. For instance, France established a national ethics committee specifically focused on AI and digital technologies. This body's role is to advise the government on ethical matters, review AI-related policies, and engage in public education efforts.

In the United States, industry-specific regulations have emerged to address AI deployment in sensitive sectors. The Food and Drug Administration (FDA), for example, has guidelines for AI applications in healthcare, ensuring that AI systems used in diagnosing or treating patients meet safety and efficacy standards. Such targeted regulations help to address domain-specific concerns while allowing room for further innovation and development.

Industry Standards and Self-Regulation

While governmental oversight is crucial, the rapidly advancing AI landscape often requires more agile approaches. Industry standards and self-regulation provide a complementary layer of governance that enables faster adaptation to new challenges and technological breakthroughs.

Industry groups and tech companies themselves often take the lead in developing standards for AI ethics. The Partnership on AI, an influential consortium of tech giants, academia, and non-profit organizations, exemplifies this approach. By bringing together diverse stakeholders, the Partnership on AI develops best practices and guidelines that encourage transparency, fairness, and accountability in AI technologies. Companies participating in such initiatives commit to adhering to these standards, influencing the broader industry to follow suit.

Additionally, self-regulation through internal ethics boards within companies like Google and Microsoft ensures that AI projects undergo ethical review before deployment. These internal bodies assess AI applications for potential biases, privacy concerns, and societal impacts, providing an early checkpoint that aligns innovation with ethical principles.

Dynamic and Adaptive Frameworks

Given the evolving nature of AI technologies, governance frameworks must also be dynamic and adaptable. Continuous evaluation and revision are necessary to keep pace with technological advancements and emerging ethical dilemmas. This adaptability requires an iterative approach, whereby feedback and insights gained from AI deployment inform the refinement of governance strategies.

One notable example of this is the UK's efforts to create an "AI code" that evolves alongside the technology. The UK government has committed to reviewing the code annually, offering a flexible governance model that can adjust to new challenges and opportunities in AI. Such adaptive frameworks ensure that governance structures remain relevant and effective, providing stability and predictability without stifling innovation.

Case Study: AI Governance in Practice – The Case of Autonomous Vehicles

To illustrate how governance frameworks for ethical AI come to life, let us consider the case of autonomous vehicles (AVs). The development and deployment of AVs present a complex interplay of ethical, legal, and technical challenges, requiring robust governance frameworks to navigate.

Countries like Germany have established comprehensive regulatory frameworks that address the ethical implications of AV deployment. The German Ethics Commission on Automated and Connected Driving, an interdisciplinary body comprising legal experts, ethicists, and technology specialists, issued a report outlining 20 ethical guidelines for AVs. These guidelines emphasize the prioritization of human life over property in accident scenarios, a principle that aligns with broader societal values.

Moreover, industry players in the AV sector have forged alliances to develop industry-wide safety standards. The AV industry consortium, led by companies like Waymo and Uber, has established principles focusing on safety, transparency, and public engagement. These principles outline their commitment to rigorous testing, clear communication with stakeholders, and the development of AVs that prioritize passenger and pedestrian safety.

Finally, adaptive frameworks are evident in the testing and deployment phases of AVs. Regulatory bodies in jurisdictions such as California have implemented flexible rules that allow for the piloting of AVs under controlled conditions. These regulatory sandboxes enable companies to iterate rapidly, testing new technologies and approaches while ensuring compliance with evolving safety and ethical standards.

By examining how these frameworks work in practice, we see the importance of comprehensive governance models that incorporate international agreements, government regulations, and industry standards. As we transition into the concluding discussion on cultivating collaboration in AI governance, let us carry forward these insights, emphasizing the collective efforts required to align AI technologies with human values in a rapidly changing world.

Cultivating a Collaborative Approach to AI Governance

In the evolving world of artificial intelligence, the pursuit of ethical governance transcends a solitary endeavor; it requires a dynamic, collective effort. This subchapter delves into the need for a collaborative approach to AI ethics and governance, emphasizing the importance of involving multiple stakeholders. The diverse perspectives from technologists, policymakers, ethicists, academics, industry leaders, and the global public are not just beneficial—they are essential. Together, these varied inputs can forge comprehensive policies that ensure AI systems are deployed with human welfare, equality, and fairness as priorities.

It is essential to recognize that the complexity of AI technologies means no single entity can foresee all possible outcomes. AI possesses the dual capability to drive unparalleled advancements or, if misapplied, exacerbate disparities and ethical issues. Thus, a collaborative approach is not only about functional integration but about creating resilient ecosystems where AI can flourish responsibly.

The Role of Multi-Stakeholder Involvement

Initiating dialogue among diverse stakeholders facilitates the identification of shared objectives and the resolution of conflicting interests. Each group brings unique expertise and priorities to the table:

- Technologists focus on the innovation, design, and deployment of AI systems. Their input ensures that AI capabilities are aligned with ethical considerations and are adeptly implemented.

- Policymakers strive to construct regulatory frameworks that manage the implications of AI while fostering innovation. Their challenge is to remain flexible enough to adapt regulatory frameworks as AI evolves.

- Ethicists and Academics provide critical analyses of AI's potential societal impact, advocating for considerations that transcend profit and productivity to encapsulate humanitarian concerns.

- Industry Leaders bring insights from practical applications of AI, illustrating the balance between commercial interests and public welfare. Their involvement also helps bridge theoretical policies with real-world implications.

- The General Public deserves a voice since they are ultimately the end-users and beneficiaries of AI systems. Ensuring that AI benefits are widely distributed prevents the exacerbation of existing inequities.

This multi-stakeholder approach reinforces the importance of diverse voices in policy construction. This inclusivity promotes transparency and builds systems that align with public values, fostering higher trust levels.

Facilitating Dialogue and Building Consensus

Facilitating meaningful dialogue requires creating platforms where these stakeholders can engage in continuous and constructive discussions. Collaboration can be fostered through organized forums, workshops, and think tanks dedicated to AI governance. For instance, multi-disciplinary conferences and public consultations are effective means of gathering diverse perspectives and developing well-rounded, applicable policies.

Consider the example of the Asilomar AI Principles, which were crafted during a conference organized by the Future of Life Institute. It brought together AI researchers, leading scientists, and other stakeholders to draft consensus-driven foundations for AI ethics and governance. This collaborative endeavor produced 23 guiding principles that outline diverse issues from research transparency and data rights to value alignment and future goals of AI systems. By fostering ongoing conversations, the Asilomar Principles demonstrate how diverse inputs can lay a foundation for future policy decisions in AI ethics.

Promoting Shared Understanding

To derive a cohesive understanding, all involved parties must comprehend basic AI principles and their implications. Shared learning initiatives, such as joint workshops or interdisciplinary education programs, can help bridge knowledge gaps. Additionally, fostering partnerships with academic institutions can enhance stakeholders' understanding of AI, equipping them to make informed decisions.

Another effective strategy is drafting foundational documents that articulate a shared vision of AI governance. For instance, the AI policy guidelines drafted by the Organization for Economic Co-operation and Development (OECD) are supported by over 40 countries and provide a standardized framework around which national policies can be tailored. This ensures that participating nations and their respective sectors operate from a common baseline, facilitating easier integration of AI systems.

Case Study: The European Union's Approach to Collaborative AI Governance

The European Union (EU) offers a pragmatic case study of how multi-stakeholder engagement fosters AI policies that are both robust and flexible. The EU's collaborative initiatives involve consultations with industry experts, public feedback mechanisms, and contributions from various civil society organizations. The EU's High-Level Expert Group on Artificial Intelligence exemplifies this approach, including participants from governments, academia, industry, and beyond to draft comprehensive AI strategies and policy recommendations. These collaborative efforts resulted in the establishment of the EU's guidelines for trustworthy AI, which emphasize respect for law and human rights, technical robustness, privacy, and accountability.

Moreover, the EU's AI Strategy prioritizes inclusive growth, ensuring that AI developments benefit society as a whole. It offers a model of how international collaborations can drive significant progress towards ethical AI governance.

Practical Application: A Global AI Observatory

One innovative idea for ongoing multi-stakeholder collaboration is the creation of a Global AI Observatory. Such an institution could serve as a centralized platform for sharing insights, resources, best practices, and governance models worldwide. By harnessing the collective expertise of various sectors, the Observatory could identify trends and provide foresight into AI's future trajectories. It would allow for dynamic policy adaptations based on real-time developments and global discourse.

Through annual reports, conferences, and online platforms, stakeholders could engage with each other, ensuring transparency and accountability while driving AI governance policies. Information sharing would promote global synchronization of ethical practices in AI, mitigating the risks of uneven regulatory landscapes.

The establishment of such a collaborative body would emphasize shared responsibility, acknowledgment that the governance of AI is an ongoing, evolving challenge—one best met through global cooperation and shared efforts.

As we prepare for the chapter conclusion, it's vital to recognize that the collaborative approach we advocate isn't merely a theoretical notion but an actionable strategy. It enables stakeholders to co-create AI systems that reflect and respect democratic values, enhancing the potential impact of AI on society and ensuring that technological growth is in harmony with human progress.

As we conclude Chapter 9, the vital tapestry of ethics and governance within the AI landscape unfurls before us as both a challenge and an opportunity. At its core, ethical AI development insists on aligning emerging technologies with human values, underscoring our shared moral responsibilities. Transparency and accountability bolster this foundation by fostering trust and ensuring that AI systems remain reliable and just, navigating the vulnerabilities inherent in privacy and data security.

Through our exploration of governance frameworks, we recognize the power of international cooperation and diverse perspectives in shaping adaptable and effective AI policies. Only by embracing a collaborative approach can we craft a governance structure that honors the dynamic nature of AI, safeguarding the principles of democracy and human welfare.

Reflecting on these critical insights, we are reminded that the journey of integrating AI into our societal fabric is not solely a technological endeavor. It requires the conscientious involvement of every stakeholder—technologists, policymakers, ethicists, and citizens—to innovate responsibly and ethically.

Thus, I invite you, the reader, to take these concepts beyond these pages and into your professional and personal realms. Engage thoughtfully and critically with the technologies you encounter, contribute meaningfully to dialogues on AI ethics, and become a steward of the values we aim to protect and promote in this emerging digital era.

As my journey with this book concludes, your exploration

continues. Take the concepts you've absorbed here as a guiding light, empowering you to actively participate in the co-creation of a future where AI serves as a true partner in human flourishing. The symbiotic relationship between intelligence and ethics is the cornerstone of the new horizon we collectively venture toward.

CONCLUSION

As we arrive at the culmination of our exploration into the compelling world of "Symbiotic Intelligence," it is essential to distill the transformative insights we've gathered throughout this journey. By unraveling the complexities and nuances of artificial intelligence, this book has sought to reshape our perception of AI from a daunting force into a collaborative partner that holds the power to amplify the human experience. From historical underpinnings to futuristic visions, we have traversed a landscape marked by technological milestones, myth-busting realities, and symbiotic advancements across industries.

In exploring these themes, we have unearthed several key strategies that form the pillars of this new era of human-AI collaboration. By understanding the evolution of intelligence, we paved the way for embracing AI's true nature—dispelling misconceptions and instead viewing it as an enabler of human potential. We delved into the building blocks of AI technology, offering a foundation for understanding its core functionalities. Through vivid examples across healthcare, education, the arts, and the workplace, we witnessed AI's transformative impact and its boundless potential to enhance productivity, creativity, and collaboration.

These insights were not just academic or theoretical. They

represented a call to arms for leveraging AI to enrich our professional and personal lives. Imagine a future where healthcare becomes increasingly proactive, enabling professionals to offer personalized medicine; where education is tailored to each learner, fostering an inclusive and dynamic learning environment; where artists transcend traditional limits, and the workplace transforms, offering new opportunities alongside machines. These concepts are not just distant possibilities but tangible actions waiting for your initiative.

Now is the moment to take that first crucial step toward integrating these strategies into your life. I invite you to embrace your role as an architect of change—actively participating in shaping a balanced, equitable, and empowered AI-driven future. Whether you are a professional in an industry on the cusp of transformation or an individual intrigued by the promise of AI, your journey begins with curiosity and a willingness to adapt and innovate.

As we stand on the brink of this revolutionary era, let us carry forward a message of optimism and aspiration. In harnessing the symbiotic potential of AI, we are not only expanding our horizons but also redefining them to create a future where technology enhances our humanity, rather than diminishes it. May you move forth with purpose and passion, inspired to act boldly and compassionately as a pioneer, forging not just advancement but a legacy of collective growth and understanding.

Together, let us craft a legacy where the synergy between human ingenuity and artificial intelligence becomes a beacon of hope for generations to come. Let's embrace the AI-driven world not as a future to fear, but as a vibrant arena where collaboration fosters progress and empowers us all.

Acknowledgments

As I conclude this journey of penning "Symbiotic Intelligence: Redefining Humanity Through AI Collaboration," I find myself reflecting deeply on the dedication and passion that have fueled this endeavor. This work is the result of countless hours of exploration and introspection, aiming to illuminate paths that can help others grow and redefine the interface between humanity and technology. I wish to express my heartfelt gratitude to everyone who has been part of this extraordinary journey.

I am profoundly indebted to the thought leaders and pioneers whose ideas and innovations have left an indelible mark on this field. Visionaries like Alan Turing, whose foundational theories in computation laid the groundwork for modern AI, inspire me daily. Also, Dr. Fei-Fei Li's work on human-centered AI has taught me to view technology with an empathetic lens, reminding me of the profound impact of integrating human values with advanced intelligence. Their work has been a beacon, guiding my vision and infusing this book with insights that I hope will resonate with readers.

This book would not have been possible without the unwavering support of my family and friends. My deep appreciation goes to my partner, whose constant encouragement and belief in my vision have been a cornerstone of my perseverance. To my friends, who have offered not only their time but their understanding as I navigated the complexities of melding technology with humanity.

A special note of thanks to my incredible editorial team, whose sharp insights and attention to detail have elevated the narrative, ensuring the clarity and accessibility I aspired to achieve. Your passion and commitment have been vital in transforming this manuscript into a work I am truly proud of.

In closing, I encourage you, dear reader, to pause and honor those who inspire you. Reflect on the people and the luminaries who have shaped your journey. Success is a mosaic of shared dreams, perseverance, and insights from those who dared to push the boundaries. It is my hope that this book sparks a dialogue that celebrates collaboration and uncovers new possibilities for synergy between humans and machines.

Author Biography

Jonathan C. Harrington stands at the nexus of technology and human imagination, a pioneering voice in digital innovation whose career serves as a testament to his unwavering passion and visionary insights. Born into the dynamic environment of San Francisco—a city renowned for its technological advancements—Jonathan's early life was woven with the rhythms of computers and emerging digital systems. This childhood fascination matured into a profound intellectual pursuit, leading him to the hallowed halls of Stanford University, where he honed his expertise with a degree in Computer Science. His academic curiosity expanded further as he pursued an MBA, combining technical prowess with strategic acumen.

Throughout his literary journey, Jonathan has become a trusted authority for his ability to demystify complex technological landscapes. His debut book, "AI Unleashed: The Future of Human-Machine Collaboration," established him as a compelling voice by illuminating how AI can augment human potential across diverse industries. This was followed by "Decoding Blockchain: Unlocking the Next Digital Revolution," where his narrative finesse empowered readers to navigate the emerging blockchain terrain. His subsequent work, "Digital Transformation Playbook: Mastering Change in the New Tech Era," solidified his role as an architect of digital strategy, providing businesses with transformative insights and tools to thrive amidst rapid technological change.

In "Symbiotic Intelligence: Redefining Humanity Through AI Collaboration," Jonathan marries his rich personal experiences with his profound professional evolution. His writing bridges tradition and innovation, offering readers a roadmap to the possibilities that lie at the intersection of human ingenuity and technological advancement. Whether he is guiding businesses through digital transformation or individuals toward a deeper understanding of AI's potential, Jonathan's narrative is a beacon of knowledge and inspiration, motivating global audiences to embrace a future where human creativity and machine intelligence coexist harmoniously.

Sources of Content

The content of "Symbiotic Intelligence: Redefining Humanity Through AI Collaboration" draws from a rich tapestry of sources, meticulously woven together to offer a comprehensive exploration of the human-AI relationship. At its core, the book is grounded in Jonathan C. Harrington's extensive experience and deep-rooted expertise in the field of digital innovation. His professional journey has been marked by a hands-on understanding of the principles that govern technological advancement and its intersection with human potential. This foundation is complemented by an in-depth analysis of industry trends and real-world applications, providing readers with relevant and actionable insights.

The book's strategic outlook is shaped by rigorous examination of contemporary practices, business models, and sector-specific strategies across various industries. By dissecting how different sectors integrate AI into their operations, Jonathan delivers a multidimensional perspective that caters to a wide spectrum of interests. This analysis is further enhanced by generative tools like ChatGPT, which contribute a data-driven layer of insight, based on a wealth of relevant sources and case studies.

This fusion of Jonathan's personal experiences, professional insights, and structured AI editorial development results in a narrative that is both engaging and practical. By harnessing the synergy between his authoritative voice and cutting-edge AI tools, "Symbiotic Intelligence" offers a powerful narrative designed to inspire and instruct, inviting readers to explore the transformative potential of AI in a forward-looking, dynamic world.

www.ingramcontent.com/pod-product-compliance
Lightning Source LLC
LaVergne TN
LVHW052057060326
832903LV00061B/3323